试点探索广西农民合作社
发展新路径

世界银行贷款广西贫困片区农村扶贫试点示范项目图册

广西壮族自治区乡村振兴外资项目发展中心　编

广西科学技术出版社
·南宁·

图书在版编目（CIP）数据

试点探索广西农民合作社发展新路径：世界银行贷款广西贫困片区农村扶贫试点示范项目图册：汉文、英文 / 广西壮族自治区乡村振兴外资项目发展中心编.—南宁：广西科学技术出版社，2024.6
ISBN 978-7-5551-2222-7

Ⅰ.①试… Ⅱ.①广… Ⅲ.①世界银行贷款—农村—扶贫—项目管理—广西—图集 Ⅳ.①F323.8-64

中国国家版本馆CIP数据核字（2024）第112215号

SHIDIAN TANSUO GUANGXI NONGMIN HEZUOSHE FAZHAN XIN LUJING
试点探索广西农民合作社发展新路径
SHIJIE YINHANG DAIKUAN GUANGXI PINKUN PIAN QU NONGCUN FUPIN SHIDIAN SHIFAN XIANGMU TUCE
世界银行贷款广西贫困片区农村扶贫试点示范项目图册

广西壮族自治区乡村振兴外资项目发展中心　编

策　　划：唐　勇

责任编辑：罗　风　　　　　　　　　　责任校对：吴书丽

美术编辑：韦娇林　　　　　　　　　　责任印制：陆　弟

出 版 人：梁　志　　　　　　　　　　出版发行：广西科学技术出版社

社　　址：广西南宁市东葛路66号　　　邮政编码：530023

网　　址：http://www.gxkjs.com　　　　编辑部电话：0771-5880461

印　　刷：广西昭泰子隆彩印有限责任公司

开　　本：787 mm×1092 mm　　1/12

字　　数：129千字　　　　　　　　　　印　　张：18

版　　次：2024 年 6 月第 1 版　　　　　印　　次：2024 年 6 月第 1 次印刷

书　　号：ISBN 978-7-5551-2222-7　　　定　　价：248.00 元

编 委 会

前　言

　　世界银行贷款广西贫困片区农村扶贫试点示范项目（简称"世行片区项目"）是广西第一个单省世行贷款扶贫项目，项目总投资约 11 亿元人民币，其中利用世行贷款资金 1 亿美元。世行片区项目覆盖区域包括百色市田东县、平果市、乐业县、田林县，河池市宜州区、东兰县、巴马瑶族自治县、凤山县、都安瑶族自治县、大化瑶族自治县，覆盖 72 个乡镇 141 个行政村，其中 127 个为贫困村（现为脱贫村），总人口 32.3 万，其中建档立卡贫困人口约 10.9 万（2017 年数据，现已全部脱贫）。世行片区项目以农民专业合作社为主要载体，通过试点示范价值链开发模型，实现提高农户增收机会的目标，建设内容包括提高面向贫困的价值链，完善公共基础设施建设及提升公共服务水平，提高对贫困地区的投入，项目管理、监测评估与学习等 4 个分项目。截至 2024 年 6 月，世行片区项目在百色、河池两市 10 县（市、区）支持建设农民专业合作社 129 个，带动合作社成员 1.6 万户，其中脱贫户 1 万户。世行片区项目在助力脱贫攻坚和乡村振兴的过程中，创新形成区域综合发展、全产业链打造、全过程监测管理等农民合作社发展经验，并取得积极成效。

　　为更好地总结和展示世行片区项目成果，广西壮族自治区乡村振兴外资项目发展中心特编撰本图册。本图册分为项目概况、项目成效和各项目县（市、区）情况 3 个部分，从项目背景、管理架构、建设内容、经验做法和创新点等方面，展现项目的实施情况和成果影响（扫描正文二维码可观看更多相关视频）。希望本图册为当前的乡村振兴工作提供有益的参考和启示。

目 录

第一章

项目概况

项目背景和概况

　　广西壮族自治区是中国5个自治区之一，有壮、汉、瑶、苗、侗等12个世居民族，位于华南地区，毗邻粤港澳，面向东南亚，是21世纪海上丝绸之路的重要枢纽，在国家对外开放大局和西部大开发战略格局中具有独特地位。自2011年启动新一轮扶贫开发以来，广西农村贫困人口由2010年的1012万减至2014年底的538万，扶贫开发工作取得了阶段性成效。但由于农村贫困面大、贫困人口多、贫困程度深的状况仍然存在，因此广西是中国脱贫攻坚的主要省区之一。

　　为深入贯彻落实《中国农村扶贫开发纲要（2011—2020年）》，实现打赢脱贫攻坚战、2020年与全国同步全面建成小康社会的宏伟目标，广西把脱贫攻坚作为头等大事和第一民生工程，举全区之力推进减贫工作。在国家发展和改革委员会、财政部、国家乡村振兴局（原国务院扶贫开发领导小组办公室）的指导下，广西与世界银行合作实施世界银行贷款广西贫困片区农村扶贫试点示范项目（简称"世行片区项目"），以试点方式示范价值链发展模式，增加农民收入，促进包容性创新发展。项目自2014年开始设计，实施期为2017年6月19日至2024年6月30日。世行片区项目不仅服务于中国脱贫攻坚战略，也符合世界银行2013—2016财年国别合作伙伴战略要求，并将短期扶持和长期发展措施、农户自我发展和增强利益联结工作结合起来，助力广西巩固拓展脱贫攻坚成果同乡村振兴有效衔接。

项目总投资

★ 项目总投资约 **11** 亿元，包括世界银行贷款资金 **1** 亿美元、国内配套资金 **4.42** 亿元。

¥ 国内配套资金
4.42 亿元

¥ 世界银行贷款资金
1 亿美元

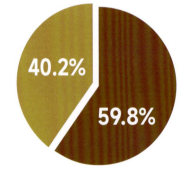

40.2%

59.8%

项目覆盖区域

★ 项目惠及广西 **10** 个县（市、区）**72** 个乡镇 **141** 个行政村，其中 **127** 个为贫困村（现为脱贫村）。

建档立卡贫困人口
约 **10.9** 万人（2017年）

覆盖总人口 **32.3** 万人

项目大事记及管理组织架构

1. 项目大事记

2014 年 11 月 24—28 日	世界银行派出项目预识别团到达广西；广西外资扶贫项目管理中心派员共同深入田东县、都安瑶族自治县实地考察。
2015 年 4 月	世界银行项目识别团与广西壮族自治区发展和改革委员会、财政厅、扶贫办等部门进行座谈，并赴乐业县和东兰县田间考察。
2015 年 10 月	世界银行项目准备考察团赴凤山县、巴马瑶族自治县、平果县实地考察，与广西深入探讨项目设计参数、项目实施和资金安排。
2016 年 3 月 21—25 日，4 月 18—29 日	世界银行预评估团与广西讨论项目文件和活动计划，其间到巴马瑶族自治县实地考察。
2016 年 6 月 20 日—7 月 1 日	世界银行评估团与广西外资扶贫项目管理中心就项目结果框架指标进行讨论，其间到田林县和田东县开展实地考察并审查县级可行性研究报告。
2016 年 11 月 30 日	世界银行出具项目评估文件。
2017 年 2 月 27 日	财政部与世界银行签订《中华人民共和国与国际复兴开发银行贷款协定（广西贫困片区农村扶贫试点示范项目）》，自治区人民政府与世界银行签订《中华人民共和国与国际复兴开发银行项目协议（广西贫困片区农村扶贫试点示范项目）》（简称"《项目协议》"）。
2017 年 4 月 7 日	世行片区项目启动会在平果县召开，时任自治区副主席黄日波、世界银行中蒙韩局副局长阿洛乌阿出席会议并致辞。阿洛乌阿女士高度肯定广西工作，在致辞中提到："自治区层面管理层和项目办是一个非常有能力的队伍，希望把广西壮族自治区项目办这种高能力运作方式引进到中国其他省份的项目管理领域中。"
2017 年 5 月	自治区扶贫开发办公室举办世行片区项目 2017 年度采购和合作社管理培训班。
2017 年 6 月 19 日	《项目协议》生效实施。
2017 年 7 月	世界银行技术团赴广西开展项目工作，审查讨论商业孵化中心、企业配套赠款等项目安排，其间实地考察田林县、田东县、都安瑶族自治县、河池市宜州区项目情况。
2017 年 9 月	经广西壮族自治区人民政府批准，建立世行片区项目建设工作厅际联席会议制度，自治区扶贫开发办公室成立世行片区项目自治区项目办公室（简称"自治区项目办"）。自治区项目办联合自治区财政厅举办世行片区项目 2017 年度财务管理和提款报账培训班。
2017 年 10 月	自治区扶贫开发办公室印发《世界银行贷款广西贫困片区农村扶贫试点示范项目实施管理手册》。

2017 年 11 月 19—30 日	世界银行第一次实施支持团赴广西开展项目工作，其间实地考察大化瑶族自治县、东兰县和平果县项目情况。
2018 年 5 月 28 日—6 月 2 日	世界银行第二次实施支持团赴广西开展项目工作，其间实地考察田东县和都安瑶族自治县项目情况。
2018 年 10 月	自治区项目办在平果县举办世行片区项目现场观摩交流暨培训班，项目管理信息系统、财务及采购管理培训班。
2018 年 11 月 26 日—12 月 9 日	世界银行第三次实施支持团赴广西开展项目工作，其间实地考察巴马瑶族自治县、凤山县和田林县项目情况。
2019 年 1 月	自治区项目办组织开展 2018 年度项目财务检查及项目调研指导，组织企业配套赠款评审专家库专家进行专题培训。
2019 年 3 月	自治区项目办举办世行片区项目合作社培训和能力建设培训班。
2019 年 6 月 24 日—7 月 5 日	世界银行第四次实施支持团赴广西开展项目工作，其间实地考察大化瑶族自治县、东兰县和凤山县项目情况。
2019 年 7 月	自治区项目办组织开展 2019 年度上半年项目财务检查及项目调研指导。
2019 年 10 月	自治区项目办举办世行片区项目管理培训班。
2019 年 11 月 4—19 日	世界银行第五次实施支持团赴广西开展项目工作，其间实地考察平果县、田东县、河池市宜州区和大化瑶族自治县项目情况。
2020 年 1 月	自治区项目办举办 2020 年度项目管理培训班，组织开展 2019 年度项目财务检查、第三方监测及项目调研指导。
2020 年 5 月 11—22 日	世界银行第六次实施支持团受新冠疫情影响，通过线上方式开展工作，委托自治区项目办实地考察大化瑶族自治县、东兰县和田东县项目情况。
2020 年 7 月	自治区项目办组织开展 2020 年度上半年项目财务检查、第三方监测及项目调研指导。
2020 年 10 月	自治区项目办开展项目中期调整相关工作。
2020 年 10 月 19 日—11 月 1 日	世界银行第七次实施支持团赴广西开展项目工作和中期检查，其间实地考察平果市、大化瑶族自治县、巴马瑶族自治县和东兰县项目情况。
2021 年 1 月	自治区项目办举办 2021 年度项目管理培训班，组织开展 2020 年度项目财务检查、第三方监测及项目调研指导。

2021 年 6 月 21—26 日	世界银行第八次实施支持团赴广西开展项目工作，其间实地考察乐业县和凤山县项目情况。
2021 年 7 月	自治区项目办组织开展 2021 年度上半年项目财务检查、第三方监测及项目调研指导。
2021 年 12 月 13—17 日	世界银行第九次实施支持团赴广西开展项目工作，其间实地考察河池市宜州区项目情况。
2022 年 1 月	自治区项目办举办 2022 年度项目管理培训班，组织开展 2021 年度项目财务检查、第三方监测及项目调研指导。
2022 年 6 月 20—23 日	受新冠疫情影响，世界银行第十次实施支持团，通过线上方式开展项目工作。
2022 年 7 月	自治区项目办组织开展 2022 年度上半年项目财务检查、第三方监测及项目调研指导。
2022 年 9 月	世行片区项目在河池市宜州区召开现场推进会。
2022 年 12 月 20—23 日	受新冠疫情影响，世界银行第十一次实施支持团，通过线上方式开展项目工作。
2023 年 1 月	自治区项目办举办 2023 年度项目管理培训班，组织开展 2022 年度项目财务检查、第三方监测及项目调研指导。
2023 年 4 月	自治区项目办组织召开商业孵化中心系列咨询服务研讨会。
2023 年 6 月 12—16 日	世界银行第十二次实施支持团赴广西开展项目工作，其间实地考察河池市宜州区、田东县项目情况。
2023 年 7 月	自治区项目办组织开展 2023 年度上半年项目财务检查、第三方监测及项目调研指导。
2023 年 11 月	"全过程支持桑蚕产业价值链，助力蚕农可持续增收致富——河池市宜州区执行世界银行贷款广西贫困片区农村扶贫试点示范项目示范案例"荣获"第四届全球减贫案例征集活动"最佳减贫案例。
2023 年 12 月 4—8 日	世界银行第十三次实施支持团赴广西开展项目工作，其间实地考察田林县和都安瑶族自治县项目情况。
2023 年 12 月—2024 年 1 月	自治区项目办组织开展 2023 年度项目财务检查、第三方监测及项目调研指导。
2024 年 2 月	自治区项目办举办 2024 年度项目管理培训班。
2024 年 4 月	"拔山见海·春意都安"世行片区项目 2024 年农民专业合作社及中小企业农特产品产地直销活动在广东省深圳市举办。
2024 年 5 月 13—17 日	世界银行第十四次实施支持团 / 完工团到广西开展工作，其间到东兰县实地调研。
2024 年 6 月 30 日	项目贷款关账。

谋篇布局

4月，世行片区项目管理和设计培训会召开

3月，世行片区项目预评估团（第一阶段）开展调研，自治区项目办及百色市、河池市项目办相关负责人参加

2015年

2016年

1月，世行片区项目投资计划编制暨合作社组建（改建）业务培训班举办

4月，世行片区项目预评估团（第二阶段）座谈会

11 月，广西和世界银行代表在北京
进行项目谈判并签约

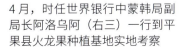
2017 年

6 月，世界银行评估团到田林县开展
实地考察

4 月，时任世界银行中蒙韩局副
局长阿洛乌阿（右三）一行到平
果县火龙果种植基地实地考察

组织实施

4月7日，世行片区项目启动会在平果县召开，时任自治区副主席黄日波、世界银行中蒙韩局副局长阿洛乌阿出席会议并致辞

10月21日，自治区项目办在平果县举办世行片区项目第一次现场观摩交流暨培训班

2017年　　**2018**年　　**2019**年

9月，世行片区项目2017年财务管理和提款报账培训班举办

11月，世界银行第一次实施支持团到田林县检查指导。下图为世界银行项目顾问约瑟夫在芒果基地前与田林县项目办人员交谈

6月，世界银行第四次实施支持团考察凤山县总结反馈会

10 月，世行片区项目中期报告会召开

9 月，自治区农业农村厅副厅长刘康（时任自治区乡村振兴局总经济师）（左二）到平果市合作社实地调研

5 月 10 日，世行片区项目视频调度会召开

2020 年　　　　　　**2021** 年　　　　　　**2022** 年

10 月，自治区项目办开展世行片区项目中期调整研讨会召开

9 月，世行片区项目在河池市宜州区召开现场推进会

4月，自治区项目办组织召开商业孵化中心系列咨询服务研讨会

6月，世界银行第十二次实施支持团到广西河池市宜州区富鑫源种养农民专业合作社实地调研。上图为世界银行项目经理陈那（右二）考察合作社农产品香水柠檬

2023年

4月，世行片区项目农民专业合作社及中小企业农特产品产地直销活动在南宁市三街两巷举行

6月，世界银行第十二次实施支持团到广西田东现代农业投资有限责任公司考察芒果干生产

12月，世界银行第十三次
实施支持团启动会召开

2月，世行片区项目管理培
训班举办

2024年

12月，世界银行第十三次
实施支持团到田林县商业
孵化中心实地调研

4月，"拔山见海·春意都安"
世行片区项目2024年农民
专业合作社及中小企业农
特产品产地直销活动在广
东省深圳市举办

2. 项目管理组织架构

　　根据项目组织实施和管理需要，成立自治区、市、县三级项目管理机构。自治区成立项目厅际联席会议，其下成立自治区项目办公室，设在自治区乡村振兴局（原自治区扶贫开发办公室），由广西壮族自治区乡村振兴外资项目发展中心（原广西外资扶贫项目管理中心）负责具体项目实施管理。项目所在设区市成立市级项目办公室，设在各市乡村振兴局，负责市级项目具体事务，督促、指导并检查所辖项目县（市、区）实施项目情况。项目县（市、区）成立领导小组和技术（专家咨询）委员会，负责领导、协调和提供技术支持。县级项目办公室设在各县（市、区）乡村振兴局，负责具体项目组织、实施和管理。

项目管理组织框架图

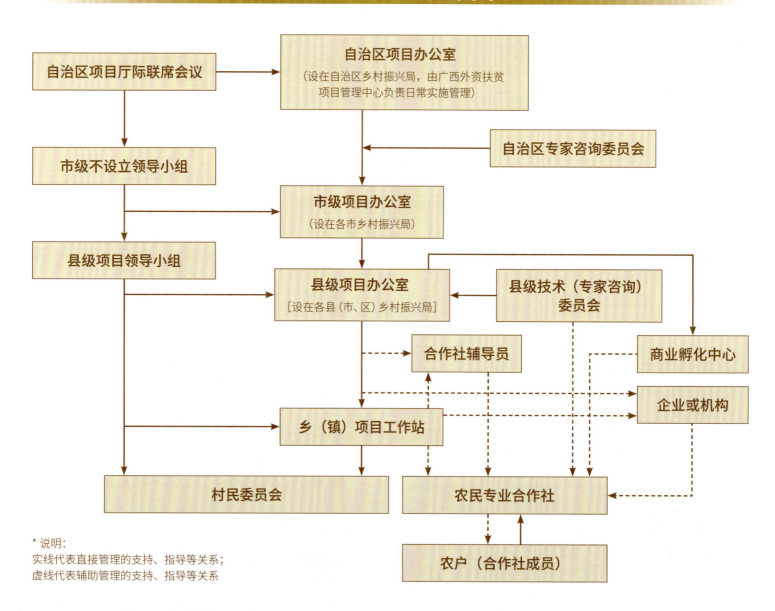

* 说明：
实线代表直接管理的支持、指导等关系；
虚线代表辅助管理的支持、指导等关系

第二章

项目成效

项目建设成果

分项目一：提升面向贫困的价值链

　　该项目旨在探索解决农业和非农业农村价值链开发及重要产业发展过程中市场失灵的问题，提高选定的农民合作社在经济活动中所创造的价值。它包含两个子项目：合作社发展基金、企业配套赠款。

2016 年 4 月，世界银行贷款所略乡平六村农村扶贫试点项目参与式规划暨合作社组建会议召开

1. 合作社发展基金

　　为新建的或已有的合作社提供赠款资金，主要用于帮助合作社增加生产附加值，并提供相应的配套设施、小型基础设施、货物、技术辅助设施，以及开展合作社能力建设，重点关注增强合作社的组织机构和管理能力，鼓励妇女作为个体积极参与合作社活动。项目合作社在技术专家、农业企业和县级政府部门的帮助下制订合作社投资计划，经自治区项目办和县级项目办评估和审批通过后，负责具体实施投资计划，开发价值链。

2017 年 11 月，世界银行第一次实施支持团专家在南宁组织开展合作社投资计划书座谈会

田东县祥周镇联强种养农民专业合作社芒果丰收

广西平果睿衍养殖农民专业合作社养殖的黑山羊

乐业县森森生态肉牛养殖专业合作社养殖场

田林县新台种养农民专业合作社成员正在榨油

河池市宜州区高寿桑蚕养殖专业合作社桑蚕养殖基地

东兰县江洞油茶农民专业合作社油茶丰收

凤山县郎里村宏翔养殖专业合作社进行山茶油辣椒酱制作

都安盛兴生态养殖专业合作社养牛场

大化岩滩仙旺农民专业合作社分红现场

巴马景丰种养农民专业合作社成员会议

2. 企业配套赠款

为独立有资质的企业或与农民合作社建立合作关系的企业提供不超过项目投资计划书总额30%的配套赠款。经透明评估和竞争优选，支持企业通过投资活动加强与合作社和农户的利益联结共享，在保障所有权的同时发挥企业示范带动作用，推动私人投资活动更具公益特性。

项目共有 12 家企业
累计获得项目赠款资金
6559.06 万元

企业自筹资金投入
17984.80 万元

带动
336 个关联合作社和村集体

约 **10** 万户农户

发展地方特色产业

获得项目赠款企业（广西鲜友农业开发有限公司）生产的产品

获得项目赠款企业（广西田林县鑫福源山茶油开发有限公司）生产的产品

获得项目赠款企业（广西乐业华东投资有限公司）康辉肉牛养殖基地展厅

获得项目赠款企业（广西嘉联丝绸股份有限公司）生产车间

获得项目赠款企业（广西五和博澳药业有限公司）生产的产品

获得项目赠款企业（广西东兰花神丝绸有限公司）生产车间

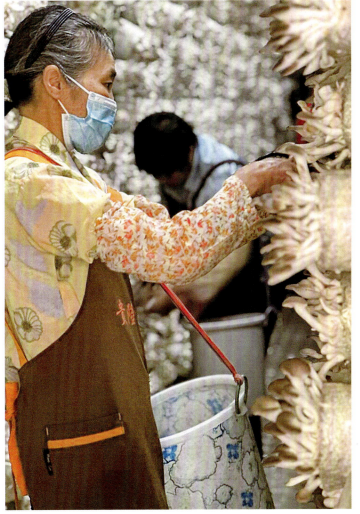

获得项目赠款企业（广西东兰贵隆生态农业科技有限公司）的智慧移动出菇房

获得项目赠款企业（广西河丰药业有限责任公司）展厅展品

获得项目赠款企业（广西巴马八百里农业有限公司）巴马生态肉牛产业核心示范区

获得项目赠款企业（广西巴马小谷鸡养殖有限公司）屠宰车间

获得项目赠款企业（广西凤山县佳弘种苗有限公司）种植基地

获得项目赠款企业（广西大化桂通农林发展有限公司）建设的鸡舍

分项目二：完善公共基础设施建设，提升公共服务水平

该项目用于支持分项目一中与价值链／重点产业发展相关的公共基础设施的建设和公共服务水平的提升。它包含两个子项目：农村基础设施建设、产业链风险管理。

1. 农村基础设施建设

围绕合作社和产业发展，完善农村基础设施建设，提升公共服务水平，为各项目村解决了生活和生产中用水难、用电难、农产品运不出去等问题。

截至 2023 年底，已在 139 个项目村建成

★ 通屯道路和生产道路

528 条 | **835** 千米

★ 水柜

531 个 | **60551** 立方米

★ 水利灌溉渠道

46 条 | **56** 千米

19

田林县旧州镇那度村油茶产业基地砂石路建设项目

世行片区项目配套资金实施的河池市源元种养专业合作社产业道路硬化项目

凤山县更沙顺发农民专业合作社蓄水池建设中（左）和竣工后（右）　　　　凤山县合胜农副产品加工专业合作社厂房建设中（左）和竣工后（右）

2. 产业链风险管理

用于支持项目县开发价值链，制订和实施包括生产风险、市场风险、金融风险等的产业综合风险评估和缓解措施。

截至 2024 年 4 月底

39 项
绿色食品认证

5 项
有机产品认证

2 项
地理标志产品认证

1 个
良好农业规范认证

1 项
"圳品"认证

25 个
食品生产许可证

10 个
富硒产品认证

8 项
有机转换认证

4 项
零碳农场认证

95 个
93 家合作社获得注册商标

提高市场竞争力

支持合作社

支持 **7** 个项目县的食品安全监督管理部门
使用项目资金采购食品安全检测监测相关设备

提高食品安全检测能力

支持 **59** 个合作社
购买农业保险

投保金额累计达
216.69 万元

/ 涉及种类包括 /

牛　羊　猪　鸡　资产设备　芒果、柑橘、百香果等果树

提升抗风险能力

绿色食品证书　　　　　　富硒农产品认定证书　　　　　巴马瑶族自治县乡村振兴研究院工作人员在进行食品安全检测

凤山县原生山茶油种植专业合作社山茶油生产

分项目三：提高对贫困地区的投入

该项目通过支持现有和新办经济实体，如小微企业、返乡农民、合作社等，提高和刺激对农村地区的投入。

都安瑶族自治县世行片区项目商业孵化中心展示厅

1.商业孵化中心

支持每个县（市、区）成立1个商业孵化中心，服务县域经济发展，为中小企业、农民专业合作社、返乡创业者、致富带头人等服务对象提供技术培训、法律援助、金融支持、专家咨询和市场营销等区域性专业化咨询服务，同时还建设世行片区项目商业服务中心网站、App和微信公众号等专业服务工作平台，更好地了解用户诉求及解决痛点问题。

世行片区项目通过商业孵化中心

开展	◆ 种植养殖技术培训 ◆ 经营管理培训 ◆ 电商直播培训	累计培训 **6896** 人次	为 **69** 家合作社	提供财务管理服务，提升农户、合作社、当地企业经营管理能力
组织	合作社和企业在南宁、桂林、深圳等地举办农产品展销会	**10** 次		促进合作社、企业在展销中与其他企业、个人达成合作意向，拓宽销售渠道

世行片区项目 2023 年十县（市）域特色农产品展销会

2. 改善融资渠道

支持各县（市、区）与当地金融机构合作，建立农户和合作社综合信用评级体系，开展农村资产评估。通过农村资产确权评估，成为个体农户和合作社从指定的金融机构获得贷款的条件。

截至 2024 年 4 月底

已经完成农户信用评级 **119903** 户

7 个县的 **16050** 户农户和 **6** 个合作社向银行申请贷款

125 家合作社开展资产评估服务

获得贷款总金额 **9.44** 亿元

资产评估服务

分项目四：项目管理、监测评估与学习

该项目用于加强和提高自治区、市、县各级项目管理机构和人员的管理能力及技术水平，建立监测评估和影响评价体系，引入专业的外部监测机构，支持日常监督、进度监测、竣工验收和安保措施的监督与监测，并从试点项目中获得经验。

截至 2023 年底，自治区项目办和各县级项目办累计举办培训班 143 期，参训 7565 人次；累计组织到贵州、云南、湖南、福建、甘肃、浙江等地学习考察 52 次共 892 人次，借鉴先进地区合作社建设、持续运营的经验和做法。

世行片区项目 2023 年度项目管理培训班

乐业县世行片区项目提升合作社能力建设考察学习

都安瑶族自治县世行片区项目办到贵州考察学习

赴江苏省举办世行片区项目 2023 年乡村振兴与农业产业发展培训班

项目经验做法及创新点

　　世行片区项目以产业为抓手，以农民合作社为主要载体，坚持以回答好"五个问题"为导向，探索脱贫地区乡村产业发展新机制、新模式。世行片区项目支持产业链发展全过程，利用参与式方法组织农户成立合作社，通过电商等方式拉近合作社与市场的距离，引入激励机制加强企业与合作社的利益联结，用较少的项目资金撬动更多的社会资本参与产业发展，推动乡村产业价值链提升、产业链延长，促进项目区产业可持续发展和农户可持续增收。

一、钱怎么用——以目标为导向，做好系统设计安排

1. 明确项目目标

★
总目标

> **示范价值链模型，增加农户增收机会**

3 个
核心指标

> 合作社盈利数量、获得产品认证和品牌数量、合作社成员数量

4 个
中级指标

> (1) 提升面向贫困的价值链
> (2) 完善公共基础设施建设与提升公共服务水平
> (3) 加大对贫困地区的投入
> (4) 项目管理、监测和学习

10 项
具体指标

> (1) 获得合作社发展基金（累计）的合作社数量；
> (2) 合作社管理效率（METT）平均得分；
> (3) 采纳创新营销实践活动的合作社成员人数；
> (4) 客户对项目提供的农村基础设施的满意度；
> (5) 开发风险管理规划的价值链数量（累计）；
> (6) 项目管理人员解决或改善不满或投诉的情况；
> (7) 客户对商业孵化中心服务的满意度；
> (8) 项目村中接受信用评级的农户数量（累计）；
> (9) 专题研讨会和会议的开展情况；
> (10) 与项目有关的出版或发表文章产出数量。

2. 围绕目标分配资金

项目资金紧密围绕实现项目目标来分配。各子项目资金按照重要性和对目标的贡献大小进行分配。

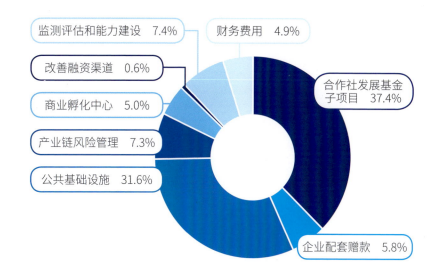

监测评估和能力建设　7.4%
财务费用　4.9%
改善融资渠道　0.6%
合作社发展基金子项目　37.4%
商业孵化中心　5.0%
产业链风险管理　7.3%
公共基础设施　31.6%
企业配套赠款　5.8%

3. 滚动安排项目规划、计划

项目时间跨度 6 年，每年制订年度项目计划，并根据实施情况进行微调。

2022 年 8 月，自治区项目办组织百色市、河池市和 10 个项目县（市、区）项目管理人员研究讨论年度项目计划执行情况和调整安排

4. 提高项目资金管理信息化水平

运用项目管理信息系统（PROMIS）对资金运行、提款报账进行管理。

项目管理信息系统（PROMIS）界面

二、事怎么做——以规范为导向，精细化管理项目全过程

1. 出台详细指导文件

自治区项目办组织编制《项目操作手册》《采购管理手册》《财务管理手册》《农民专业合作社操作指南》《商业孵化中心操作运行指南》《企业配套赠款子项目管理办法》等文件，为规范管理和执行项目提供指导。

2. 事前审查项目方案

建立项目投资计划书（实施方案）审查机制，通过审查后的项目才能实施。例如企业配套赠款项目，按照"二审一查一公示"程序严进严管：

"二审" 是指符合资质要求的企业按照规定格式提交项目投资计划书后，须通过两轮评审。第一轮由县级项目办组织专家评审和实地核验，专家组出具评审通过意见后报县人民政府批准。第二轮由自治区项目办组织专家评审和实地核验，专家组针对投资计划的带农益农效益、创新性、附加值创造潜力、技术和财务可行性、可持续性、环境影响等方面进行评分。

"一查" 是指自治区项目办将通过第二轮评审的项目投资计划书报送世界银行审查。

"一公示" 是指项目投资计划书通过世界银行项目团队审查后，将拟支持企业名单和资金挂网公示 7 天。

通过"二审一查一公示"程序后，企业才能获得赠款资金支持。

《关于世界银行贷款广西贫困片区农村扶贫试点示范项目企业配套赠款子项目拟支持的企业名单及资金公示》

企业配套赠款项目投资计划书评审会

自治区项目办组织专家到企业配套赠款项目申请企业广西东兰花神丝绸有限公司进行实地核验

3. 签订项目实施协议

将各子项目投资计划书（实施方案）按照专家组意见、建议修改后，实施主体（合作社、企业、相关机构等）与县级项目办签订实施协议，明确带农益农机制责任条款，承诺具体带贫量化指标等，并按照项目操作手册要求组织实施、采购、培训。项目资金专款专用、专账核算、专人管理，并按照报账制审核拨付。

4. 加强内部管理和外部监测

开展全过程项目管理和监测，确保进度可见、问题可控、目标可兑。一方面通过县级项目办具体管理监督、自治区项目办日常指导督查、自治区审计厅定期开展项目审计，"三管齐下"加强项目监管；另一方面由第三方独立机构根据项目实施协议和投资计划书，定期针对项目实施进度和质量、产业发展规模、产业链增值、利益联结机制建立和落实、脱贫户和监测户覆盖带动、技术支持等方面进行现场检查核验，并出具评估报告反馈自治区项目办和县级项目办，以抓好薄弱环节整改工作。

2022 年 9 月，自治区农业农村厅副厅长刘康（时任自治区乡村振兴局总经济师）实地调研河池市宜州旺腾生态农业发展专业合作社

南宁师范大学开展世行片区项目第三方监测评估工作

自治区项目办组织开展 2022 年度上半年项目财务检查

自治区项目办组织开展 2023 年度上半年项目财务检查

5. 打造专业人才队伍

一是引入专业咨询团队，为项目办和合作社提供产业发展、合作社管理、财务、采购、环境和社会安保等方面的技术指导。

二是组建项目专家库，涵盖农业经济、市场营销、食品安全、法律和融资等专业领域，通过专家审核把关企业和合作社的投资计划，避免盲目投资和无效投资。

三是培养自有人才，为每个合作社配备专门的辅导员，针对项目人员和合作社成员组织开展各类培训。

项目管理培训、采购和财务管理培训	种植养殖技术培训	经营管理培训	电商直播培训	累计参训
69 期	**31** 期	**31** 期	**12** 期	**7565** 人次

世行片区项目乡村振兴与农业产业发展培训班（第二期）

凤山县合胜农副产品加工专业合作社举行红薯种植技术培训

广西田东紫荷种养农民专业合作社法律风险防控咨询

田东县芒果专家到芒果基地进行芒果管理技术培训

三、产品怎么销——以市场为导向，提升全产业链

1. 解决种养风险问题

一是疫病防控。除常规举办种养技术培训之外，项目还支持各县（市、区）开展动物疫病防控咨询服务，充分利用专家的专业优势解决合作社遇到的难题。

二是购买保险。项目资金支持合作社购买动物、植物保险，降低合作社种植养殖风险。

畜禽疫病防控

大化七百弄康利养殖专业合作社成员和理事长在鸡舍给鸡打疫苗

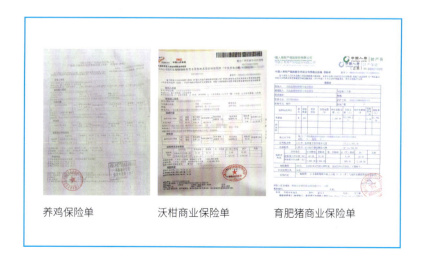

养鸡保险单　　　　沃柑商业保险单　　　　育肥猪商业保险单

2. 提升产品附加值

　　世行片区项目支持产业链延长、价值链提升，鼓励合作社在种、养、收的基础上，开展农产品加工，支持商标注册和绿色食品、有机产品及地理标志产品认证，拓展产品销售渠道，提高市场竞争力。

截至 2024 年 4 月底

☑ **25** 个合作社
获得食品生产许可证

☑ **93** 家合作社
获得注册商标

☑ 获得绿色食品、有机产品及地理标志产品等认证
共 **70** 项

凤山县郎里村宏翔养殖专业合作社生产的获得注册商标的山茶油辣椒酱

乐业县强民油茶种植农民专业合作社的山茶油绿色食品认证证书

巴马富饶油茶农民专业合作社产品获得有机产品认证证书

凤山县郎里村宏翔养殖专业
合作社获得的商标注册证

3. 提升产业竞争力

　　项目资金全过程支持宜州桑蚕、田东芒果、田林山茶油等地方优势特色产业，提升一批龙头企业深加工能力，拓宽企业市场销售渠道，提高产业链综合收益，带动合作社和农户共同受益。有 12 家企业累计获得项目赠款资金 6559.06 万元，企业自筹资金投资 17984.80 万元，带动 336 个关联合作社和村集体约 10 万户农户发展地方特色产业。

广西嘉联丝绸股份有限公司染丝车间

广西乐业县猕香果业专业合作社猕猴桃丰收

广西鲜友农业开发有限公司芒果深加工车间

4. 多渠道助力销售

建立专门面向合作社和县域小微企业的App、视频号和微信公众号，培育合作社电商直播员，搭建网络销售渠道，并通过商业孵化中心举办电商培训，搭建直播场地，组织开展产品展销会，帮助合作社和餐饮企业、连锁便利店等客户面对面交流对接，促进销售意向达成。

世行商业服务中心官方网站
网址：http://www.gxshfh.cn/serviceHall

世行商业服务中心
视频号页面

世行商业服务中心
微信公众号页面

截至 2023 年底

★ 各县（市、区）共开展电商培训 **12** 次　★ 培育学员 **529** 人

★ 建立平台账号 **204** 个　★ 协办直播 **612** 场次

销售农产品约 **6817** 单

交易额 **463** 万元

在南宁、桂林、深圳等地举办世行片区项目展销会，共有 598 家合作社、餐饮企业及农产品销售企业参加。产销双方直接对接，缩短销售环节，使合作社土特产直接面向终端消费者销售。

2023 年 4 月 28 日—5 月 1 日，都安瑶族自治县在南宁市三街两巷举办世行片区项目农产品营销对接会

四、收益怎么分——以成员为主体，保障脱贫户及妇女弱势群体利益

1. 明确股权、利润分配方案

　　合作社单个自然人成员出资占股不超过合作社成员出资总额的 30%，少数股东占有股权不超过 40%。起步阶段合作社成员不少于 30 人，脱贫户成员占比不少于 20%。项目投资方案申报阶段，严格审查利润分配方案，合作社可分配盈余的 60% 用于成员交易量返还，40% 用于股权分配，确保大多数人受益。

2. 明确联农带农责任

　　企业配套赠款投资计划书明确脱贫农户受益方式及数量指标，通过第三方专业机构定期核验完成情况，确保合作社和农户参与企业增值增收活动并获得合理的收益分配。

获得项目赠款企业（广西田林县鑫福源山茶油开发有限公司）给受雇农户签发工作证明

凤山县郎里村宏翔养殖专业合作社社员大会

广西五和博澳药业有限公司收购农户桑枝，带动农户增收

3. 项目成效可持续

项目合作社成员共 16236 人（一户一人），其中妇女成员 6787 人，占比 42.2%；脱贫人口 10316，占比 63.6%。

截至 2023 年底

妇女成员 **6787** 人
占比 42.2%

脱贫人口 **10316**
占比 63.6%

分红金额共计
768.5 万元

受益成员
（一户一人）
6892 人

受益脱贫户数
4085

项目合作社成员 **16236** 人

项目支持的 **129** 家合作社

大化岩滩仙旺农民专业合作社，妇女成员在粉碎牧草饲料

凤山县原生山茶油种植专业合作社为妇女提供就业机会

乐业县强民油茶种植农民专业合作社成员人工剥壳油茶籽

大化东皇岭农民专业合作社成员领取分红

五、资产怎么管——以产权为核心，明晰各方责任、权利和义务

 ★企业配套赠款投资形成的资产归属企业

 ★合作社发展基金投资形成的资产归属合作社

 ★明确不良资产处置，产权转移至村集体

项目赠款资金建设的生产线厂房和实验室（广西东兰贵隆生态农业科技有限公司）

项目赠款资金购买的生产设备（广西大化发瑞村跃腾农民专业合作社）

项目赠款资金购买的冷链运输车（广西巴马八百里农业有限公司）

项目赠款资金购买的生产设备（百色益亩粮仓农业发展农民专业合作社）

整体项目影响

一、项目实践成功入选全球减贫案例

项目资金支持河池市宜州区种桑养蚕农民专业合作社和以粉碎桑杆为基料的食用菌农民专业合作社，助推 1.8 万户蚕农收入可持续稳定增长。该案例入选"第四届全球减贫案例征集活动"最佳减贫案例。

项目资金全过程支持桑蚕产业价值链

桑叶种植

小蚕培育

蚕蛹结茧

收蚕茧

缫丝

丝绸产品售卖

二、项目宣传覆盖面和影响力扩大

在《经济日报》《科技日报》《农民日报》《中国县域经济报》以及广西广播电视台新闻频道《经济新观察》栏目、中国经济网、人民网等网络媒体刊发项目宣传稿件，大幅度扩大世行片区项目成效宣传的覆盖面和影响力。

世界银行项目顾问、高级农业经济学家约瑟夫先生因在世行片区项目等工作中为广西经济建设和社会发展做出重要贡献，被广西壮族自治区人民政府授予2020年度广西"金绣球友谊奖"。

广西壮族自治区乡村振兴外资项目发展中心二级巡视员李清法为约瑟夫先生代发2020年度广西"金绣球友谊奖"荣誉证书

三、项目实践经验得到推广应用

　　项目构建企业与合作社及农户利益联结机制，联农带农取得的成果、做法以及今后改进措施等情况，被《广西政协信息》第116 期刊登，并获得自治区领导批示。项目创新实践和管理模式经验不仅被借鉴应用于广西脱贫攻坚和乡村振兴工作，还在中国首个援外扶贫项目——东亚减贫示范合作技术援助项目中得到推广应用，为讲好中国减贫故事、分享中国减贫经验做出贡献。

东亚减贫示范合作技术援助项目援助对象——老挝琅勃拉邦市象龙村的村民在用参与式方法设计村内产业发展项目

借鉴世行片区项目公示公告制度，东亚减贫示范合作技术援助项目在老挝琅勃拉邦市象龙村活动中心外墙设置公告栏，公示项目建设内容和资金使用情况

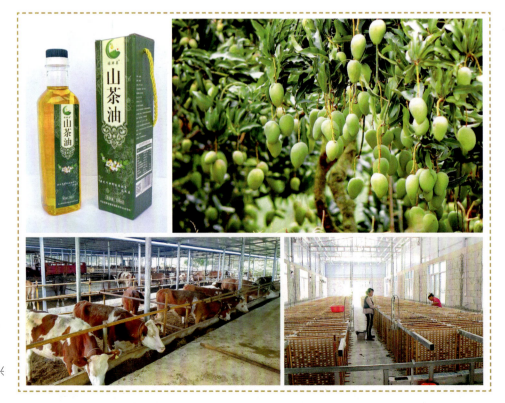

项目支持产业发展，助力广西脱贫攻坚和乡村振兴部分成果展示

第三章

项目县（市、区）情况

田东县
世行片区项目情况

项目概况

百色市田东县位于广西西南部，曾是国家扶贫开发工作重点县。2017年，田东县启动实施世行片区项目。

2019年，田东县实现脱贫摘帽。

田东县世行片区项目区域共覆盖7个乡镇14个行政村，分别是祥周镇联合村，林逢镇民族村，思林镇良余村、定阳村、新圩村，印茶镇那板村、僚坤村、立新村，作登瑶族乡新安村、大板村、陇祥村，那拔镇福星村、六洲村，义圩镇那荷村，其中13个为贫困村（现为脱贫村）。

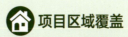

🏠 项目区域覆盖

7 个乡镇　**14** 个行政村　其中 **13** 个贫困村（现为脱贫村）

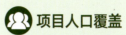

👥 项目人口覆盖

总人口 **37994** 人

其中建档立卡贫困人口 **18659** 人（2017年）

少数民族人口 **33055** 人　妇女人口 **20244** 人

田东县世行片区项目投资金额情况

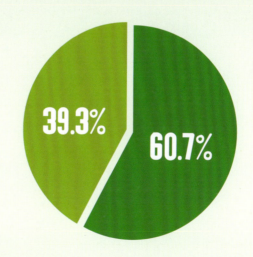

39.3%　60.7%

¥ 国内配套资金　**4420.0** 万元

¥ 世界银行贷款资金　**6827.4** 万元

项目成效

截至 2023 年底

企业与田东县签订联结协议

26 家

8 家为项目合作社

带动农户

5899 户

其中脱贫户

1423 户

超过监测目标值

753 户

企业收购芒果

10400 吨

芒果汁产量

5800 吨

一、建立三方利益联结机制，企业带农益农成效明显

　　广西鲜友农业开发有限公司是田东县实施世行片区项目企业配套赠款项目的企业。该公司采用"公司＋合作社＋农户／脱贫户"的带农益农的联结机制，与合作社及农户开展种植、采收、储运、加工等环节的全面合作。按照"底价保障，市价保收"协议收购合作社及成员的芒果次果（次果占比 20% ～ 30%，仅外观和大小逊色于商品果，但市场销售渠道少），为当地果农拓展水果市场销售渠道，增加农户收益，巩固脱贫成果。同时，企业完善和延伸水果产业链，增加果品附加值，促进田东县水果产业可持续发展，取得了推动振兴乡村产业，带动农户增收、企业增效、政府财税增收的综合效果。

芒果加工车间

芒果加工企业带动农户增收受益

广西鲜友农业开发有限公司芒果深加工基地工作现场

二、促进合作社可持续发展，有效提升产业附加值

1. 开展基础设施建设

截至 2023 年底，已在 14 个项目村建成

46 条，**52.694** 千米　通屯道路和生产道路

119 个，**4297.6** 立方米　水柜

合作社鸭舍建设中（上）和竣工后（下）

2. 增设专家咨询服务

建立田东县商业孵化中心专家信息库和潜在服务对象信息库，为合作社发展提供芒果种植、种桑养蚕、营销、法律等专业技术支持。

☆对各合作社开展定向服务 **116** 次

☆面向社会开展各种咨询服务 **12** 次

田东县商业孵化中心财务专家到良余村进行现场培训、指导工作

田东县组织芒果专家对种植户进行技术指导

3. 开展农产品认证，加强产业链风险管理

项目支持 6 个合作社获得绿色食品认证，支持合作社开展农产品包装设计和商标注册、购买商业保险等，提升合作社产品的市场竞争力和风险防范力，并完成农户信用评级 4009 户、合作社资产评估 14 家。

✔ ☆完成农户信用评级 **4009** 户

✔ ☆合作社资产评估 **14** 家

田东县加强产业链风险管理（田东县食品药品检测所）

广西田东县创富种桑养蚕专业合作社不断提升产品风险防范力

广西田东县紫荷种养农民专业合作社

4. 加强能力建设，拓宽销售渠道

　　田东县商业孵化中心组织开展种植养殖技术培训、经营管理培训、电商直播培训等，累计培训 979 人次，提升了农户、合作社和当地企业的经营管理能力；组织参加农产品展销会；组织合作社和企业到区内外考察学习、交流合作 28 次，促进合作社、企业与其他企业、个人达成合作。

组织参加农产品展销会

促进

芒果收入 **37.11** 万元

山茶油收入 **3.2** 万元

蚕茧收入 **11.59** 万元

田东县世行片区项目组织外出考察

5. 收获诸多荣誉称号

　　在世行片区项目的支持下，田东县聚福园现代农业种植养殖农民专业合作社 2019 年被评为百色市农民示范合作社，2020 年被评为自治区级示范社，2022 年被评为国家级示范社；广西田东县创富种桑养蚕专业合作社、田东县祥周镇联强种养农民专业合作社在 2021 年均被评为百色市农民示范合作社。

广西田东县创富种桑养蚕专业合作社所获荣誉

平果市

世行片区项目情况

项目概况

　　百色市平果市位于广西西南部，地处滇桂黔石漠化片区。2017 年，平果县（于 2019 年 12 月 26 日撤县改市）启动实施世行片区项目。

　　平果市世行片区项目区域共覆盖 8 个乡镇 11 个行政村，分别是新安镇坡南村，果化镇巴龙村、布荣村，太平镇临林村、茶密村，海城乡拥齐村，坡造镇龙板村，旧城镇新更村、六岸村，凤梧镇龙排村，榜圩镇永旺村。

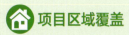 项目区域覆盖

8 个乡镇　　**11** 个行政村均为贫困村（现为脱贫村）

项目人口覆盖

总人口 **21220** 人

其中建档立卡贫困人口 **6294** 人（2017 年）

少数民族人口 **21032** 人　　妇女人口 **7317** 人

平果市世行片区项目投资金额情况

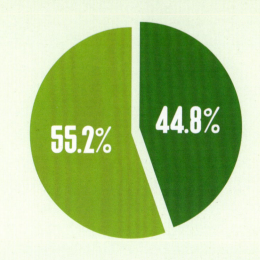

55.2%　　44.8%

¥ 国内配套资金
4420.0 万元

¥ 世界银行贷款资金
3592.4 万元

项目成效

截至 2023 年底

建成生产便道	架设电杆
28 条	**95** 根
总长 **32.18** 千米	电线 **13309.7** 米

惠及

35851 人

建成排水沟	建成水池（水塔）
9 条	**14** 个
6604.48 米	**2194.47** 立方米

一、高效推进农村公共基础设施建设，改善合作社生产条件

　　截至 2023 年底，建成生产便道 28 条，总长 32.18 千米；架设电杆 95 根、电线 13309.70 米；建成排水沟 9 条，总长 6604.48 米；建成水池（水塔）14 个，总容量 2194.47 立方米；惠及 35851 人。

广西平果睿衍养殖农民专业合作社电力设施施工前（左）和竣工后（右）

平果市世行片区项目太平镇吉林村龙仇产业路建设工程施工前（左）和竣工后（右）

二、构建合作社及农户利益联结机制，促进当地特色产业发展

1. 增加农户土地收入

合作社在项目实施区

涉及农户
537 户

租赁土地
810.95 亩*

农户获得土地租金
76.38 万元

平果市绿然生态农业专业合作社向农户发放土地租金

平果市凤英生态农业专业合作社向农户发放土地租金

2. 增加劳务协作收入

优先聘请合作社成员到合作社务工，共带动成员 225 户，成员获得收入 185.43 万元。

平果市凤英生态农业专业合作社成员通过给桑叶施肥管护获得务工收入

广西平果市农东种养专业合作社成员通过收割牧草增加收入

---

* 非法定计量单位，1 亩 ≈ 666.67 平方米。

3. 上门收购农产品实现双赢

合作社上门采购成员、农户的玉米、大豆等农产品用于畜禽养殖，共采购农产品 22.25 吨，支付费用 6.68 万元，增加了成员、农户的收入。

采购农产品

22.25 吨

支付费用

6.68 万元

平果富恒飞肉鸽养殖农民专业合作社上门收购农户的玉米

4. 提供服务降成本

合作社向成员提供农业生产资料的购买和农产品的销售、加工等服务，以节省交易费用、减少生产支出。

截至 2023 年底，平果市项目合作社合计发展成员 1433 人，其中脱贫户成员 834 人；合作社饲养肉牛 740 头，种牛 115 头，新生牛犊 34 头；饲养种羊 356 只，新生羊羔 300 只；饲养种鸽 5300 对，青年鸽 2200 对，乳鸽 11635 只；管护牧草 1250 亩，管护桑园 134 亩。项目资金支持建设的 9 个合作社年产值达 671.48 万元。

广西平果市农东种养专业合作社养牛场

平果市拥民种养农民专业合作社牛犊采购讨论会

三、针对性开展能力建设，提升项目参与方可持续发展能力

1. 提升可持续发展能力

　　截至 2023 年底，平果市项目办组织商业孵化中心人员、合作社辅导员及合作社管理人员等 8 批 161 人次，分别到南宁、河池、崇左、凭祥、乐业以及贵州、云南等区内外考察学习。开展合作社采购、财务、运营管理、畜禽养殖技术等培训 14 期，培训人员 782 人次，进一步提升合作社自我组织、自我管理、自我监管的可持续发展能力。

平果市项目办赴崇左市、凭祥市考察学习交流

2. 提升经营管理能力

　　项目支持成立平果市商业孵化中心，为平果市小微企业、合作社的发展和创业起步提供服务。截至 2023 年底，通过开展产业技能培训、财务管理培训、经营管理培训，累计培训 432 人次，提供服务 97 次，提升了农户、合作社及当地小微企业的经营管理能力。

平果市世行贷款项目商业孵化有限公司项目合作社产业技能培训

四、加强产业链风险管理，提升农产品市场竞争力和风险防范力

　　截至 2023 年底，通过项目资金支持，平果市项目合作社 7 个产品、14 个商标完成设计与注册，7 个养殖合作社聘请了畜禽疫病防控服务机构，为 1913 头牛羊购买了商业保险。

畜禽疫病防控专家到平果巴岭农业专业合作社开展疫病检测与养殖技术指导

商标注册

乐业县
世行片区项目情况

项目概况

百色市乐业县位于广西西北部，地处滇桂黔石漠化片区，是龙滩库区县、革命老区县、有机农业基地示范县，曾是国家扶贫开发工作重点县、深度贫困县。2017年，乐业县启动实施世行片区项目。

2020年，乐业县实现脱贫摘帽。

乐业县世行片区项目区域共覆盖6个乡镇12个行政村，均为贫困村（现为脱贫村），分别是同乐镇达存村、刷把村，甘田镇达道村、板洪村，逻沙乡塘英村、全达村，新化镇林立村、那社村，花坪镇花岩村、运赖村，逻西乡七更村、民治村。

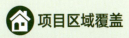

项目区域覆盖

6个乡镇　**12**个行政村均为贫困村（现为脱贫村）

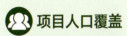

项目人口覆盖

总人口 **24186** 人

其中建档立卡贫困人口 **11827** 人（2017年）

少数民族人口 **10641** 人　妇女人口 **10598** 人

乐业县世行片区项目投资金额情况

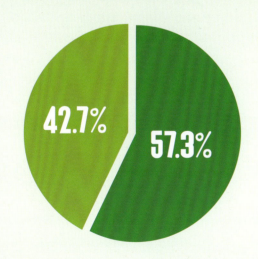

42.7%　　**57.3%**

¥ 国内配套资金 **4420.0** 万元　　¥ 世界银行贷款资金 **5930.1** 万元

项目成效

截至 2023 年底，项目共支持建设合作社 12 个，吸纳成员 1870 人，其中脱贫户成员 1250 人，妇女成员 829 人。

项目支持的乐业县森森生态肉牛养殖专业合作社和广西乐业华东投资有限公司、乐业县草王山茶业有限公司、乐业县恒源生态农业综合开发有限公司 3 家农业龙头企业获得"广西现代特色农业示范区"称号。乐业县家佳香山茶油农民专业合作社获得"广西农民专业合作社示范社"称号。

一、发挥项目资金辐射带动作用，促进企业和合作社联农带农发展

项目带动 12 家合作社和 3 家企业开展猕猴桃种植 1374 亩、油茶种植 10833 亩、茶叶种植 956 亩、肉牛养殖 1150 头，水溶肥加工每年 8000 吨、有机茶叶深加工每年 500 吨。

12 家合作社 **+ 3** 家企业

投资总额 **10350.1** 万元

合作社成员 **1870** 人 ➡ 其中脱贫户成员 **1250** 人

乐业县家佳香山茶油农民专业合作社获得"广西农民专业合作社示范社"称号

乐业县家佳香山茶油农民专业合作社的山茶油被评为"名优农产品重点推荐品牌"

二、选好扶持产业项目，大力发展绿色农业、循环农业

1. 发展绿色产业

　　项目支持在乐业县猕猴桃主产业园中心区域建设水溶肥生产加工厂，与乐业县肉牛养殖基地（包括1家世行片区项目支持的养牛专业合作社）、固体有机肥料厂无缝对接，将乐业县固体有机肥料厂产生的废水、当地畜牧养殖的粪便、糖厂的糖泥等作为原料，通过粉碎、混合、反应、包装等精加工工艺流程，变废为肥，生产出符合国家标准的有机水溶肥，用于全县脱贫奔康产业园和猕猴桃、茶叶等种植专业合作社及种植农户改善土壤性质，提高产品质量，打造乐业县绿色、有机、循环产业。

广西乐业恒源生态农业综合开发有限公司生产的有机水溶肥

2. 荣获专业认证

　　截至2023年底，12家项目合作社中：

10 家获得绿色食品认证

5 家获得有机转换产品认证

2 家获得地理标志认证

12 家合作社均获得商标注册证书

7 家加工类合作社获得食品生产许可证

乐业新宇种植专业合作社的猕猴桃产品获得中华人民共和国地理标志

三、完善基础设施及配套，提升公共服务质量水平

1. 基础设施日益改善

截至 2023 年底，受益产业包括猕猴桃 5321 亩、油茶 7488 亩、八角 2521 亩、茶叶 1732 亩、畜牧 2040 头（匹）。

乐业县逻沙乡全达村产业路

截至 2023 年底，项目支持的村级公共基础设施建设项目覆盖

乡镇 **6** 个，项目 **12** 个　　道路 **36** 条

储水池 **17** 座　　排洪道 **1** 条

受益农户　　　　　　　脱贫户
3272 户 **14697** 人　　**2027** 户 **9547** 人

2. 增设公共服务及相关配套

项目支持成立乐业县商业孵化中心，为现有企业的发展和创业起步提供服务。截至 2023 年底，乐业县商业孵化中心开展种植养殖技术培训、电商直播培训，累计培训 1120 人次；完成农户信用评级 4000 户，完成合作社资产评估 12 家；帮助 3 家合作社获得货款 348.0 万元，帮助完成信用评级的 656 户农户向信用社贷款共计 4246.8 万元。

乐业县逻西乡七更村油茶种植第一期实用技术培训

四、加强项目内部管理，培育本地人才队伍

　　乐业县商务孵化中心为每个合作社配备专门的辅导员，辅助合作社制订和执行项目投资计划；聘用专业财务人员，加强合作社财务管理；截至 2023 年底，组织县项目办和合作社骨干开展项目实施管理培训、考察 3 期，培训 74 人次，提升相关人员的项目管理和自我发展能力。

乐业县世行片区项目提升合作社能力建设考察学习开班典礼

乐业县振兴源种养专业合作社成员接受培训后开始操作设备加工茶叶

乐业县世行片区项目提升合作社能力建设考察学习培训班

田林县

世行片区项目情况

项目概况

百色市田林县位于广西西北部，是国家乡村振兴重点帮扶县，地处滇桂黔石漠化片区，境内以山地为主，曾是国家扶贫开发工作重点县。2017 年，田林县启动实施世行片区项目。

2019 年，田林县实现脱贫摘帽。

田林县世行片区项目区域共覆盖 10 个乡镇18 个行政村，均为贫困村（现为脱贫村），分别是百乐乡板干村、根标村，利周瑶族乡平布村，乐里镇文化村，八渡瑶族乡博峨村、者塘村，者苗乡八中村、八亨村，潞城瑶族乡三瑶村、弄光村，旧州镇徕周村、示甫村、那度村，六隆镇平细村，浪平镇小坳村，定安镇八新村、八来村、常井村。

🏠 项目区域覆盖

10 个乡镇   **18** 个行政村均为贫困村（现为脱贫村）

👥 项目人口覆盖

总人口 **27563** 人

其中建档立卡贫困人口 **12745** 人（2017 年）

少数民族人口 **20944** 人   妇女人口 **11672** 人

田林县世行片区项目投资情况

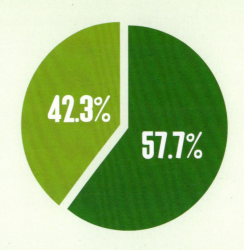

42.3%   57.7%

¥ 国内配套资金
4420.0 万元

¥ 世界银行贷款资金
6031.2 万元

项目成效

田林县平布村达康种养专业合作社茶油果

项目通过企业配套赠款支持广西田林县鑫福源山茶油开发有限公司升级设备、提高产能

一、结合当地资源、规划，选择发展产业类型

　　田林县山地资源丰富，有"中国油茶之乡"的美誉，当地群众发展意愿强烈。项目支持的 12 家合作社中有 10 家是油茶产业，项目还通过企业配套赠款支持广西田林县鑫福源山茶油开发有限公司升级设备、提高产能，契合《广西壮族自治区国家乡村振兴重点帮扶县巩固拓展脱贫攻坚成果同乡村振兴有效衔接实施方案》的田林油茶主导产业链规划。该企业与 9 家合作社（其中 6 家为项目合作社）签订收购协议，2021—2023 年累计收购合作社和农户油茶籽约 5600 吨，受益农户 2239 户，其中脱贫户 550 户。

项目合作社

合作社 **12** 家

油茶合作社 **10** 家

鑫福源签订协议

合作社 **9** 家

项目合作社 **6** 家

累计收购合作社和农户油茶籽约 **5600** 吨

受益农户 **2239** 户

其中脱贫户 **550** 户

二、延长产业链，开展跨区域品牌合作

八渡笋是田林县著名特产、中国国家地理标志产品。项目支持田林兴茂八渡笋种植专业合作社将农户种植的八渡笋加工成酸笋，作为柳州螺蛳粉配料供应给相关企业，年供货95281千克，销售额28.83万元，带动成员63户，每户年均增收4500元。

田林县兴茂八渡笋种植专业合作社成员在加工八渡笋

田林县兴茂八渡笋种植专业合作社成员晾晒笋干

包装后的八渡笋产品

三、完善基础设施建设和提升公共服务水平，加强产业全链条风险管理

1. 开展基础设施建设

项目支持建设通屯道路、产业道路 43 条，总长 133.05 千米，产业区水柜 40 个，以及油茶晒场、合作社综合培训楼等。受益项目村 18 个，受益农户 3393 户，其中脱贫户 1185 户。

建设通屯道路、产业道路	产业区水柜	受益农户
43 条 **133.05** 千米	**40** 个	**3393** 户 其中脱贫户 **1185** 户

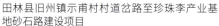

田林县旧州镇示甫村村道岔路至珍珠李产业基地砂石路建设项目

田林县旧州镇徕周村南燕沟至梅花山道路硬化工程

田林县定安镇八新村那来岔路过八轮屯至柑橘基地产业道路硬化项目

2. 加大培训力度

加强合作社能力建设。截至 2023 年底，项目组织开展电商培训、产业技术培训累计 8 期，共培训学员 659 人次。

截至 2023 年底

组织开展电商培训、产业技术培训	培训学员
8 期	**659** 人次

田林县世行片区项目 2020 年农民专业合作社经营管理能力提升培训班

3. 提升产品品质和市场竞争力

截至 2023 年底，项目支持合作社获得绿色食品认证 2 项；在县域内建设 8 个农产品检测室，以提升当地食品安全检测能力；完成 12 家合作社资产评估、4583 户农户信用评级，帮助合作社和农户改善融资渠道。

截至 2023 年底

支持合作社获得绿色食品认证	建设食品检测室	完成合作社资产评估	完成农户信用评级
2 项	**8** 个	**12** 家	**4583** 户

田林县平布村达康种养专业合作社商标注册证书

田林县市场监督管理局利周所农产品检测室

田林县市场监督管理局八桂所农产品检测室

4. 拓宽销售渠道

田林县商业孵化中心积极组织开展线下展销会。截至 2023 年底，共组织合作社和企业在南宁等地参加农产品线下展销会 8 次，促进合作社、企业在展销中与众多企业、个人达成合作意向，拓宽销售渠道。

5. 发展电商平台

田林县商业孵化中心积极开展电商销售、搭建直播场地、宣传合作社品牌。截至 2023 年底，在抖音、西瓜视频、腾讯等平台建立账号 3 个，直播近 30 场次，销售农产品 1346 单。

广西田林县鑫福源山茶油开发有限公司产品原材料采购

田林县商业孵化中心及合作公司主播直播带货

河池市宜州区

世行片区项目情况

项目概况

河池市宜州区位于广西中部偏北，是壮族歌仙刘三姐的故乡。2017年，宜州区启动实施世行片区项目。

宜州区世行片区项目区域共覆盖8个乡镇、14个行政村，分别是刘三姐镇谷洞村，洛西镇洛富村，祥贝乡里洞村、白伟村，龙头乡高寿村、龙田村，北牙瑶族乡白龙村、保康村、潘洞村、豆竹村、沙浪村，北山镇波串村，福龙瑶族乡龙侯村，庆远镇叶茂村，其中11个为贫困村（现为脱贫村）。

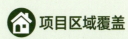 项目区域覆盖

8个乡镇　**14**个行政村　其中**11**个贫困村（现为脱贫村）

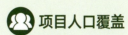 项目人口覆盖

总人口**39110**人

其中建档立卡贫困人口**9903**人（2017年）

少数民族人口**32868**人　妇女人口**19353**人

宜州区世行片区项目投资金额情况

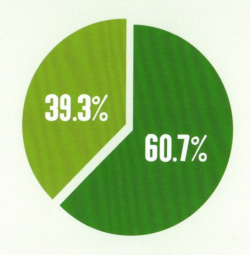

39.3%

60.7%

¥ 国内配套资金
4420.0万元

¥ 世界银行贷款资金
6827.4万元

项目成效

一、采用"合作社＋基地＋农户"经营模式促农增收

以合作社形式帮助农户扩大生产经营规模，提高农产品质量，降低生产成本，通过标准化生产示范作用、种植养殖技术培训、提供就业岗位等方式带动脱贫户增加收入。截至 2023 年底，项目共支持建设合作社 14 个，其中 5 个合作社先后被评为自治区级、河池市级示范农民专业合作社；签订合作协议合作社和村集体 38 个，带动农户 35789 人；14 个合作社增加长期用工 90 多人、短期用工 400 多人，有效增加了成员农户的就业收入。

建设合作社	示范农民专业合作社	签订合作协议合作社和村集体	带动农户
14 个 ➡	5 个	38 个 ➡	35789 人

河池市宜州区韩昌易养殖专业合作社为农户增加就业岗位

河池市宜州区韩昌易养殖专业合作社分红现场

二、提升龙头企业联农带农机制

围绕宜州区支柱产业种桑养蚕及丝绸生产，项目支持农业产业化龙头企业广西嘉联丝绸股份有限公司、广西五和博澳药业有限公司实施技改扩建，提升综合实力。截至 2023 年底，增加建筑劳务岗位 100 多个，扩大产能增加生产岗位 50 多个，以及增加较多临时用工数量。

项目采用"龙头企业 + 合作社 + 基地 + 农户（脱贫户）"合作发展模式，着力发展订单农业，大力推进标准化种桑养蚕技术示范推广应用，以工业反哺农业，加强与蚕农的利益联结，充分发挥龙头企业带动农民增收的作用。截至 2023 年底，相关企业与 38 家合作社签订合作协议，直接带动企业周边 3 万亩桑蚕基地建设，惠及农户 42284 户，其中脱贫户 7136 户。2023年收购合作社和农户蚕茧 5064.0 吨、桑枝 14465.4 吨，带动农户每亩桑枝增收 300 元。

广西嘉联丝绸股份有限公司获得项目赠款，扩大产能，增加生产岗位

企业收购合作社农户蚕茧，带动农户增收

签订合作协议合作社

38 家

带动企业周边桑蚕基地建设

3 万亩

惠及农户

42284 户

其中脱贫户

7136 户

2023 年

收购合作社和农户蚕茧

5064.0 吨

桑植

14465.4 吨

带动农户每亩桑枝增收

300 元

三、围绕产业发展改善基础设施条件

截至 2023 年底，完成公共基础设施建设项目共 104 个，其中硬化通屯道路 23 条，总长 27.71 千米；产业道路 19 条，总长 27.10 千米；安装安全防护栏 12 条，总长 13.79 千米；水柜项目 3 个；水利渠道维修项目 19 个；饮水安全保障项目 15 个；其他项目 13 个。基础设施的提升明显改善了各项目村的生产生活条件，受益村 32 个，受益农户 7906 户，其中脱贫户 479 户。

河池市宜州区龙头乡高寿村产业道路

四、加强全产业链风险管理

1. 提升食品安全监测能力

截至 2023 年底，已有 2 家合作社通过有机产品认证，2 家通过绿色食品认证。同时，项目支持宜州区食品安全监督管理单位采购食品安全检测设备，以提升其食品安全监测能力。

通过绿色食品认证的河池市宜州区兴伟种养专业合作社产品

有机产品认证证书

绿色食品证书

2. 加强技术、管理等培训

项目支持成立宜州区商业孵化中心，为现有合作社和企业的发展及创业起步提供针对性服务。截至2023年底，宜州区商业孵化中心通过开展桑蚕种养实用技术培训、经营管理培训、财务管理培训，累计培训1535人次，提升了农户、合作社、当地企业经营管理能力；积极组织有关合作社参加各县（区）开展的展销会活动9次。

河池市源元种养专业合作社举办农商联盟数字化系统培训会

3. 解决产业资金发展问题

项目结合宜州区开展的"五位一体"信用体系建设，支持宜州区与当地金融机构合作，积极开展农户信用评级和合作社的资产评估工作。高质量完成了20多个行政村农户信用评级工作，获得商业金融机构评级授信的农户2万户，其中86%的农户为优质评级，可从金融机构获得5万元贷款资金，有效解决了农户发展产业的资金瓶颈问题。

宜州区项目办聘请养殖技术人员围绕肉牛养殖产业开展课题研究，以养殖效益与生态环境和谐发展为目标，为合作社提出提升肉牛养殖效益的科学建议。相关课题研究成果为宜州区的肉牛养殖户们所用。

养殖技术人员为合作社提出肉牛养殖科学建议

河池市宜州区万家富养殖业专业合作社养殖基地

东兰县

世行片区项目情况

项目概况

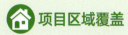

河池市东兰县位于广西西北部，地处滇桂黔石漠化片区，山多地少，群众分散居住在千山万弄中，是革命老区县，也曾是国家扶贫开发工作重点县、深度贫困县。2017年，东兰县启动实施世行片区项目。

2019年，东兰县实现脱贫摘帽。

东兰县世行片区项目区域共覆盖7个乡镇、16个行政村，均为贫困村（现为脱贫村），分别是三石镇纳腊村、纳合村、仁合村、长峒村，东兰镇江洞村、委荣村，隘洞镇板老村、同乐村、六通村、拉社村，武篆镇坤王村，长乐镇板登村，切学乡板烈村、切亨村、英西村，巴畴乡巴英村。

项目区域覆盖

7 个乡镇 **16** 个行政村均为贫困村（现为脱贫村）

项目人口覆盖

总人口 **31022** 人

其中建档立卡贫困人口 **8873** 人（2017年）

少数民族人口 **27952** 人 妇女人口 **14227** 人

东兰县世行片区项目投资金额情况

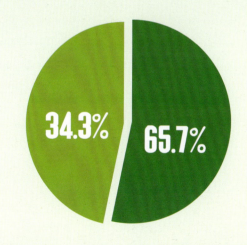

34.3% 65.7%

¥ 国内配套资金
4420.0 万元

¥ 世界银行贷款资金
8476.1 万元

项目成效

一、助力特色产业发展

1. 支持农民专业合作社和企业发展

项目支持 16 家农民专业合作社、3 家企业，通过农业支柱产业重组，打造示范种养产业园，并对现有种养产业区进行改造升级，改善落后的基础设施，推动山茶油、桑蚕、药材、食用菌、蛋鸡、肉鸡、黑山羊、肉牛等 8 个特色地方产业发展，促进产业提质增效。

东兰县江洞油茶农民专业合作社的油茶果种植基地

东兰县江洞油茶农民专业合作社的压榨设备

东兰县江洞油茶农民专业合作社山茶油成品

广西河丰药业有限责任公司展厅产品展示

广西东兰贵隆生态农业科技有限公司生产的产品——神仙山莲花菌

广西东兰贵隆生态农业科技有限公司生产的产品——木耳酱

东兰县委荣顺顺生态农业专业合作社养殖的鸡

东兰县百草园原生态山羊养殖专业合作社养殖的黑山羊

东兰县乐益种养专业合作社养殖的牛

2. 支持基础设施建设

截至 2023 年底

硬化道路	砂石路	生产便道
10 条	8 条	41 条
11.939 千米	14.997 千米	59.633 千米

引水渠道	水池建设	其他设施
3 条	25 座	23 处
2.237 千米	3610 立方米	

三石镇纳腊村蓄水池竣工验收

二、打造"企业带动 + 合作社运作 + 农户参与"模式

截至 2023 年底，获得企业配套赠款资金支持的广西东兰花神丝绸有限公司、广西东兰贵隆生态农业科技有限公司、广西河丰药业有限责任公司等 3 家企业共计与 45 个合作社和 177 个村集体签订合作协议，带动农户 19261 户。

广西东兰花神丝绸有限公司收购蚕农蚕茧

广西东兰花神丝绸有限公司的制丝车间

前往广西东兰贵隆生态农业科技有限公司出菇大棚上班的农户

三、联农带农促增收

东兰县共 16 家项目合作社，其中 15 家合作社实现分红，凸显农民增收的显著效果，有力推进乡村振兴工作。

东兰县巴畴乡巴英油茶种植合作社 2021 年度成员分红大会

项目合作社

共吸纳成员
2265 人

脱贫户
1343 人

合作社分红

受益成员
1985 人

脱贫户
1271 人

分红金额
125.44 万元

最高获得分红
7319 元

四、提升合作社产品市场竞争力和风险防范力

截至 2023 年底，项目支持合作社获得油茶食品生产许可证 3 家，获得绿色食品标志认证 8 家，获得注册商标 14 个；帮助 7 家合作社购买商业保险；为东兰县食品安全监督管理部门采购相关设备，以提升当地食品安全监测能力。

合作社产品获得的绿色食品认证证书

五、围绕产业发展提高公共服务质量

项目支持成立东兰县商业孵化中心，截至 2023 年底，累计为合作社、中小企业主、返乡创业者、致富带头人提供指导和服务 200 人次。项目支持东兰县与当地金融机构合作，开展农户和合作社综合信用评级体系和农村资产评估，截至 2023 年底，完成合作社资产评估 16 个、农户信用评级 4000 户。

东兰县商业孵化中心

★提供指导和服务 **200** 人次

☆完成合作社资产评估 **16** 个

☆农户信用评级 **4000** 户

六、加强项目管理人员能力建设

东兰县项目办开展培训 18 期，培训人数 200 人次，其中，项目办管理人员 120 人次，合作社管理人员 80 人次。通过农业产业发展培训班等培训，进一步提升东兰县项目管理人员通过建设农民专业合作社品牌来推动乡村发展、乡村建设及乡村治理的水平。

2021 年 11 月 9 日在东兰县外资中心举办畜禽疫病防控培训会

东兰县项目办组织召开三石镇纳合村桑蚕养殖专业合作社技术培训会

东兰县项目办组织召开第一期中小企业、农民专业合作社和创业带头人能力建设培训班

东兰县项目办组织专家到隘洞镇板老村牛角坡板栗林下综合养殖专业合作社召开乌鸡养殖技术培训会

巴马瑶族自治县

世行片区项目情况

项目概况

巴马瑶族自治县位于广西西北部，地处滇桂黔石漠化片区，被评为"世界长寿之乡""中国长寿之乡"，是革命老区、少数民族聚居区，曾是国家扶贫开发工作重点县。2017年，巴马瑶族自治县启动实施世行片区项目。

2020年，巴马瑶族自治县实现脱贫摘帽。

巴马瑶族自治县世行片区项目区域共覆盖7个乡镇、14个行政村，分别是巴马镇坡腾村、设长村、法福村、盘阳村、介莫村，燕洞镇岩廷村，那社乡东烈村，所略乡平六村，西山乡合乐村、弄京村，凤凰乡长和村、德纳村，百林乡罗皮村、平田村，其中9个为贫困村（现为脱贫村）。

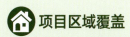

项目区域覆盖

7个乡镇　**14**个行政村　其中**9**个贫困村（现为脱贫村）

项目人口覆盖

总人口 **41053** 人

其中建档立卡贫困人口 **14002** 人（2017年）

少数民族人口 **34296** 人　妇女人口 **17714** 人

巴马瑶族自治县世行片区项目投资金额情况

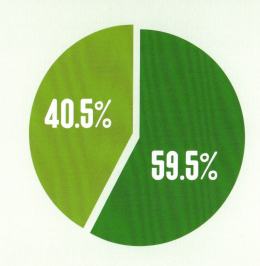

40.5%

59.5%

¥ **国内配套资金**
4420.0 万元

¥ **世界银行贷款资金**
6480.7 万元

项目成效

项目支持

14 家合作社

项目带动

2166 户 **9260** 人

其中脱贫户 **1520** 户 **6615** 人

少数民族人口 **1960** 人，妇女人口 **1033** 人

项目发展

山羊养殖

香猪养殖

羽鸡养殖

种桑养蚕

水果种植

油茶加工

寿乡牛养殖

一、示范合作社建设成果明显

截至 2023 年底，项目支持的 14 家合作社有 11 家实现盈利，获得油茶合作社食品生产许可证认证 2 个，注册商标 7 个，完成合作社 2166 户农户信用评级工作。项目实施以来实现分红的合作社有 6 家，累计分红 60 万元，其中 2023 年度已有 4 家实现分红，金额共计 30 万元，受益成员（一户一人）631 人，其中受益脱贫户 404 人。

巴马众庆种养农民专业合作社和广西巴马景丰种养农民专业合作社在 2022 年均获得自治区级农民合作社示范社荣誉称号。广西巴马福秀种养殖农民专业合作社在 2019 年被评为巴马瑶族自治县优质农民专业合作社和河池市农民专业合作社示范社。

广西巴马农旺种养农民专业合作社羊舍建设中（左）和竣工后（右）

巴马众庆种养农民专业合作社寿香牛长势良好

广西巴马景丰种养农民专业合作社林下栖息的鸡群

二、商业孵化中心提供专业化服务

项目支持成立巴马瑶族自治县商业孵化中心，为小微企业和合作社发展提供培训教学、注册登记和认证、商业管理与策划、法律咨询服务、金融服务，开办展销会、交流会等专业化服务。截至2023年底，累计开展针对性服务75次，累计服务660人次。

累计开展

针对性服务 **75** 次，服务 **660** 人次

巴马瑶族自治县商业孵化中心

2023年巴马瑶族自治县特色农产品南宁展销会活动现场

2023年巴马瑶族自治县电商直播培训班

三、企业配套赠款带动作用明显

　　巴马瑶族自治县的广西小谷鸡农牧有限公司和广西巴马八百里农业有限公司获得项目配套赠款支持，截至 2023 年底，带动关联合作社 29 家，带动 4523 户农户发展特色产业，收购合作社和农户饲养的肉鸡 64.32 万只、供应鸡苗 44.49 万羽；带动参与牧草种植、秸秆回收农户总户数达 701 户，带动脱贫户 121 户。

广西小谷鸡
农牧有限公司

广西巴马八百里
农业有限公司

获批项目
配套赠款支持

带动关联合作社
29 家

收购合作社和农户饲养的肉鸡
64.32 万只

+

带动发展特色产业
4523 户

供应鸡苗
44.49 万羽

带动农户参与牧草种植、
秸秆回收
701 户

带动脱贫户
121 户

广西小谷鸡农牧有限公司产业核心示范区

广西小谷鸡农牧有限公司生产基地

广西巴马八百里农业有限公司和牛繁育基地

四、改善项目区生产生活条件

截至 2023 年底

基础设施建设情况 »

生产道路

57 条

123.6 千米

挡土墙

2701.19 立方米

道路硬化

56.27 平方米

防护栏

3.67 千米

广西巴马福秀种养殖农民专业合作社生产道路

巴马瑶族自治县所略乡平六村油茶合作社生产道路

凤山县

世行片区项目情况

项目概况

河池市凤山县位于广西西北部，地处滇桂黔石漠化片区，曾是国家扶贫开发工作重点县和广西深度贫困县。2017年，凤山县启动实施世行片区项目。

2020年，凤山县实现脱贫摘帽。

凤山县世行片区项目区域共覆盖4个乡镇、16个行政村，分别是凤城镇弄者村，金牙瑶族乡更沙村、坡茶村、陇旺村，乔音乡那王村、合运村、上林村、同乐村、文里村，长洲镇板伦村、那爱村、那老村、那乐村、长洲村、郎里村、板任村，其中14个为贫困村（现为脱贫村）。

 项目区域覆盖

4 个乡镇　**16** 个行政村　其中 **14** 个贫困村（现为脱贫村）

项目人口覆盖

总人口 **36108** 人

其中建档立卡贫困人口 **11385** 人（2017年）

少数民族人口 **21163** 人　妇女人口 **15833** 人

凤山县世行片区项目投资金额情况

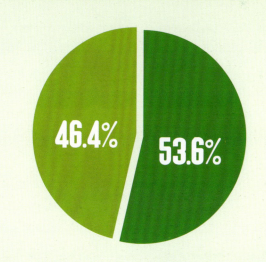

46.4%　53.6%

¥ 国内配套资金　**4420.0** 万元

¥ 世界银行贷款资金　**5106.2** 万元

项目成效

一、支持建设合作社取得积极成效

截至 2023 年底，项目共支持建设合作社 11 个，带动脱贫户 780 人，少数民族人口 924 人，妇女人口 718 人；发展了油茶加工、辣椒酱生产、大米生产加工、核桃收购加工、小蚕共育、蚕茧收购烘干、五色糯米饭制作、肉猪养殖等产业。

支持建设合作社	带动脱贫户	少数民族人口	妇女人口
11 个	**780** 人	**924** 人	**718** 人

凤山县长爱油茶加工专业合作社生产设备

凤山县农产品快检室工作人员对合作社农产品进行安全检验

凤山县佳利生猪养殖专业合作社养殖的生猪

凤山县宏星核桃农民专业合作社五色糯米饭产品

二、提供配套赠款，支持企业加强与合作社和农户的利益联结共享

项目为企业提供配套赠款，支持其通过投资活动加强与合作社和农户的利益联结共享。截至 2023 年底，签订合作协议合作社和村集体 9 个，带动农户 2252 户。

广西凤山县佳弘种苗有限公司荣誉证书墙

广西凤山县佳弘种苗有限公司收购农户十大功劳木

凤山县种植中药材功劳木示范基地

广西凤山县佳弘种苗有限公司展厅陈设

三、完善基础设施建设，提高公共服务水平

截至 2023 年底，项目支持合作社获得包括绿色食品、地理标志产品在内的农产品认证 13 项，并完成包装设计和商标注册；在江洲、平乐、长洲、砦牙、金牙、思源等镇（乡、社区）建成 6 个农贸市场特色农产品安全快速检测室，为凤山县食品安全监督管理部门采购相关设备以加强当地食品安全检测监测。

项目支持凤山县与当地金融机构合作，截至 2023 年底，已经完成农户信用评级 4400 户，完成合作社资产评估 19 家。

截至 2023 年底，已在 16 个项目村解决生活和生产用水、农产品运输难题

建成生产道路	引水渠道	蓄水池	修建油茶晒场	浆砌挡土墙
47 条	**15** 条	**217** 座	**1** 个	**168** 处
135.093 千米	**18.482** 千米	**89470** 立方米	**510** 平方米	**25562** 立方米

装屯级道路锌钢安全防护栏	路面维修	合作社场地硬化	铺设饮水管网工程	
12 条	**3** 条	**1000** 平方米	**3618** 米	
9060 米	**2343** 平方米			

2021 年 10 月 25 日竣工的乔音乡那王村巴鸦屯饮水安全巩固提升工程

良好农业规范认证证书

山茶油绿色食品认证证书

四、加强培训，提升农户、合作社、当地企业自我发展能力

　　截至 2023 年底，凤山县商业孵化中心通过开展种植养殖技术培训、财务培训、能力建设培训、自媒体培训等，累计培训 1162 人次，提升了农户、合作社、当地企业的经营管理能力。

　　项目支持本县组织人员到湖南、贵州、福建等地的世界银行项目合作社及产业基地学习考察，累计组织 118 人次，借鉴先进地区合作社建设、持续运营的经验和做法。

凤山县项目办开展合作社技术培训提升会

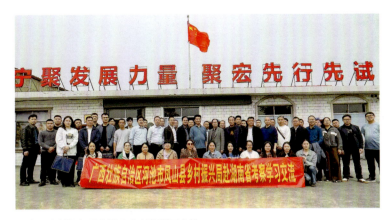

凤山县乡村振兴局赴湖南省考察学习交流

五、拓展农产品销售渠道

　　凤山县商业孵化中心组织合作社和企业在桂林、南宁举办或参加农产品线下展销会，促进合作社、企业在展销中与众多企业、个人达成合作意向，拓宽销售渠道。

　　2023 年 11 月，凤山县在桂林举办主题为"长寿食材　广西味道"的世行片区项目特色农产品展销活动暨 2023 年广西餐饮文化博览会世行项目专场推介会。

凤山县世行片区项目 2023 年特色农产品展销活动在桂林举行

都安瑶族自治县

世行片区项目情况

项目概况

都安瑶族自治县位于广西中部偏西，地处滇桂黔石漠化片区，曾是国家扶贫开发工作重点县、深度贫困县、广西极度贫困县。2017 年，都安瑶族自治县启动实施世行片区项目。

2020 年，都安瑶族自治县实现脱贫摘帽。

都安瑶族自治县世行片区项目区域共覆盖 7 个乡镇 15 个行政村，分别是澄江镇六里村、甘湾村，保安乡元力村，永安镇安乐村、永吉村，高岭镇五峒村、弄名村、复兴村、加庭村、加全村、宜江村、加茶村，龙湾乡映山村，下坳镇隆坝村，东庙乡安宁村，其中 13 个为贫困村（现为脱贫村）。

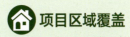

项目区域覆盖

7 个乡镇　**15** 个行政村　其中 **13** 个贫困村（现为脱贫村）

项目人口覆盖

总人口 **34447** 人

其中建档立卡贫困人口 **9950** 人（2017 年）

少数民族人口 **26072** 人　妇女人口 **12781** 人

都安瑶族自治县世行片区
项目投资金额情况

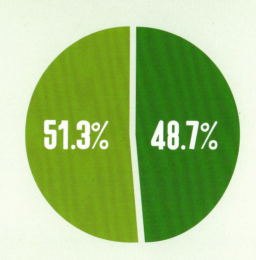

51.3%　48.7%

¥ 国内配套资金　¥ 世界银行贷款资金
4420.0 万元　**4191.0** 万元

项目成效

一、支持合作社建立农户联结发展机制

在项目支持下，合作社帮助成员建设鸡舍、羊舍、蚕房等，统一订购鸡苗，提供免费养殖技术指导等，有效帮助成员降低生产成本和风险。

项目支持建设合作社	合作社发展成员	其中脱贫户
13 个 ➡	**1485** 人	**1084** 人

💲 支持合作社产业投资方向

都安山羊养殖 **7** 个	种桑养蚕 **1** 个
肉猪养殖 **2** 个	肉牛养殖 **1** 个　瑶乡土鸡养殖 **2** 个

广西都安绿银桑蚕种养专业合作社向成员发放桑苗

广西都安百弄土鸡养殖专业合作社饲养的百弄鸡

都安盛兴生态养殖专业合作社

都安兴龙种养专业合作社的羊舍

广西都安绿银桑蚕种养专业合作社的蚕房内部

都安盛兴生态养殖专业合作社的瑶山牛

二、完善基础设施建设，提升公共服务水平

截至 2023 年底，项目为 13 个项目村建设道路、水柜，改善当地农户生产生活条件。都安瑶族自治县商业孵化中心累计开展种植养殖技术培训、经营管理培训、电商直播培训 23 期，累计培训 1077 人次，为合作社提供专业技术咨询和技术培训服务 17 次，提升了农户、合作社、当地企业的经营管理能力和产业发展信心。

道路

63 条

54.903 千米

水柜

44 个

11600 立方米

培训

23 期

1077 人次

都安瑶族自治县商业孵化中心为项目合作社聘请专职的代理记账会计员，为项目合作社进行统一财务记账工作，加强对合作社财务制度的管理，有效提高合作社管理的规范化水平。

都安瑶族自治县商业孵化中心于 2023 年 4 月 28 日—5 月 1 日在南宁市三街两巷举办世行片区项目农产品展销活动。此次展销活动主要对各县（市、区）的世行片区项目农产品和文化旅游资源进行大力宣传，促进合作社、企业在展销中与众多企业、个人达成合作意向，拓宽销售渠道。现场销售农特产品约 20 万元，签订战略合作协议 2500 万元，其中广西澳都农牧科技有限责任公司和深圳市寿乡臻品农业发展有限公司签约金额达 1000 万元。

"秀美都安　春生万物"——世行片区项目 2023 年农民专业合作社及中小企业农特产品产地直销活动

第一期牛、羊养殖技术培训班（桂合泉现场点）

高岭镇加全村下坡至弄机产业道路硬化工程

2021 年农民专业合作社第二期电商经营培训

三、畜禽疫病防控服务为合作社发展保驾护航

都安瑶族自治县项目办聘请第三方专业机构为各项目合作社提供畜禽疫病防控措施服务，对种植养殖中出现的疫病问题给予有效应对措施，减少合作社的种植养殖风险。

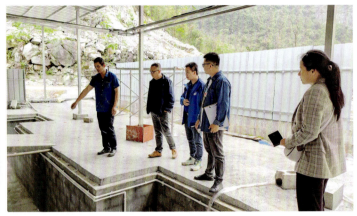

广西悦牧生物科技有限公司畜禽疫病防控及现场指导

四、改善融资渠道

项目支持都安瑶族自治县与当地金融机构合作，开展农户和合作社综合信用评级体系，聘请第三方机构开展合作社资产评估。通过信用评级及资产评估，成为个体农户和合作社从指定的金融机构获得贷款的条件。截至 2023 年底，已经完成农户信用评级的达 4053 户，完成合作社资产评估的 11 家。

资产评估服务

五、加强能力建设

截至 2023 年底，都安瑶族自治县商业孵化中心累计开展

种植养殖技术培训
经营管理培训　　**23**期 **1077**人次
电商直播培训

外出考察学习　　**7**期 **78**人次

赴贵州省考察学习

赴甘肃省世界银行项目考察学习

赴巴马瑶族自治县考察学习商业孵化中心运行情况

赴大化瑶族自治县世行片区项目考察学习

大化瑶族自治县

世行片区项目情况

项目概况

　　河池市大化瑶族自治县位于广西中部偏西北的红水河中游,地处滇桂黔石漠化片区,曾是国家扶贫开发工作重点县、广西极度贫困县。2017 年,大化瑶族自治县启动实施世行片区项目。

　　2020 年,大化瑶族自治县实现脱贫摘帽。

　　大化瑶族自治县世行片区项目区域共覆盖 8 个乡镇 11 个行政村,分别是大化镇大调村、双排村,都阳镇尚武村、忠武村、武城村,六也乡加司村,岩滩镇六说村,羌圩乡健康村,乙圩乡常怀村,七百弄乡弄雄村,江南乡发瑞村。其中 10 个贫困村(现为脱贫村)。

项目区域覆盖

8 个乡镇　　**11** 个行政村　　其中 **10** 个贫困村(现为脱贫村)

项目人口覆盖

总人口 **30128** 人

其中建档立卡贫困人口 **5406** 人(2017 年)

少数民族人口 **27879** 人　　妇女人口 **13219** 人

大化瑶族自治县世行片区项目投资金额情况

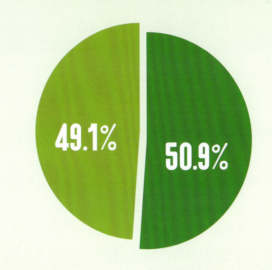

49.1%　　50.9%

¥ 国内配套资金
4420.0 万元

¥ 世界银行贷款资金
4590.5 万元

项目成效

一、完善基础设施建设，项目社会效益凸显

截至 2023 年底，已在 11 个项目村建成通屯道路和生产道路 65 条共 85.412 千米，51 个水柜共 8850 立方米，水利灌溉渠道 4 套，改善了当地村民的生产生活条件。

在 **11** 个项目村

建成通屯道路和生产道路	水柜	水利灌溉渠道
65 条	**51** 个	**4** 套
85.412 千米	**8850** 立方米	

羌圩乡健康村康志达合作社人畜饮水工程

大化镇双排村排下屯内道路硬化

七百弄乡弄雄村康利养殖专业合作社示范基地挡土墙

二、加强规范管理，合作社建设显成效

项目共支持建设合作社 11 个，截至 2023 年底，吸纳成员 1258 人（一户一人），其中脱贫人口 732 人，占比 58.19%；少数民族人口 1233 人，占比 98.01%；妇女人口 440 人，占比 34.98%。合作社通过入股分红、务工、土地租赁等方式带动成员增收，累计分红 239.61 万元，受益农户 1258 户，提供务工岗位 38 个。

项目支持建设合作社 **11** 个，吸纳成员 **1258** 人（一户一人）

其中脱贫人口 **732** 人 占比 58.19%

少数民族人口 **1233** 人 占比 98.01%

妇女人口 **440** 人 占比 34.98%

入股分红 务工 土地租赁等

累计分红 **239.61** 万元

受益农户 **1258** 户

务工岗位 **38** 个

在加强合作社规范管理方面，主要有以下做法：

一是建立合作社管理制度。明确合作社理事会、监事会运行机制，以及成员的权利和义务。

二是明晰股权。给每个成员制作和发放股权证，在合作社宣传栏公示成员情况，包括姓名、股份来源、持有股份等信息。

三是重视社务、财务公开。通过微信、宣传栏，及时主动发布合作社相关情况。

四是民主管理。用合作社成员自己的话说就是"大事由成员大会决定，小事由理事会决定"。

五是选好带头人。按照有公心、有能力、有时间的"三有"原则，由合作社成员推选出合作社管理人员。

大化弄曲种养专业合作社规章制度

大化东皇岭农民专业合作社入股社员资产分红公示

三、引入专业服务，促进产业发展提质增效

在促进产业发展提质增效方面，主要有以下做法：

一是引入专业服务。通过邀请农业专家到合作社现场指导，传授先进种植技术，实现果园管护技术标准化、规范化。

二是完善生产设备。建设安装水肥一体化滴灌设备、堆肥发酵设备、基地轮滑轨道设施等，极大地提高了生产效率。

三是改善融资渠道。截至 2023 年底，已经完成农户信用评级达 4000 户，完成合作社资产评估服务 10 家。

四是购买商业保险。截至 2023 年底，累计为 225 亩沃柑、15200 羽肉鸡、5340 头生猪、512 只羊、60 头牛等购买保险，提升了合作社风险防范能力。

农业专家现场指导种植、剪枝、病虫害治理等技术

大化东皇岭农民专业合作社堆肥棚

农村商业银行工作人员到大化瑶族自治县商业孵化中心接洽世行片区项目试点合作社融资渠道开发项目

肉牛养殖保险单和羊养殖保险单

四、开展产品认证，拓宽市场销售渠道

截至 2023 年底，通过支持合作社获得包括绿色食品认证在内的认证 4 项，以及完成包装设计和商标注册，提升了合作社的产品市场竞争能力，解决了合作社好产品卖不上好价钱的问题。例如，大化东皇岭农民专业合作社种植沃柑 225 亩，合作社 2018 年注册东皇岭沃柑商标，2019 年获得绿色食品认证，2020 年获得"圳品"认证。东皇岭沃柑销售价格比一般沃柑高 30%，销售收入逐年攀升。

截至 2023 年底，通过开展种植养殖技术培训、经营管理培训、电商直播培训累计培训 540 人次，提升了农户、合作社、当地企业的经营管理能力；组织开展线下展销会，组织合作社和企业在南宁等地举办农产品线下展销会，促进合作社、企业在展销中与众多企业、个人达成合作意向，拓宽销售渠道。

大化瑶族自治县合作社绿色食品认证证书

大化瑶族自治县都阳镇忠武村东皇岭农民专业合作社的沃柑获得"圳品"认证

五、加强人才培养，促进合作社可持续发展

大化瑶族自治县项目办累计参加和举办了 15 期项目培训，共计 600 人次；累计外出考察 2 期 56 人次，先后到湖南省、贵州省世界银行项目合作社和产业基地考察学习。

大化瑶族自治县世行片区项目代表赴湖南省考察学习

大化东皇岭农民专业合作社成员在采摘沃柑

后 记

本图册由广西壮族自治区乡村振兴外资项目发展中心组织编撰，各级项目办、田东县乡村振兴信息中心、平果市委宣传部、乐业县融媒体中心、田林县委宣传部、东兰县融媒体中心、巴马瑶族自治县文化广电体育和旅游局、都安瑶族自治县委宣传部、南宁市鸿林文化传播有限责任公司，以及获得世行片区项目支持的企业和合作社为本图册提供了丰富的图片，河池市宜州区委宣传部提供了图册封面图片。以上各单位的支持为本图册顺利编印出版奠定了坚实基础。

本图册内容涉及世行片区项目实施的方方面面，时间跨度大，编写任务重，编者能力水平亦有限，如有疏漏和不当之处，敬请广大读者批评指正。

编写组

2024 年 5 月

Pilot Exploration of New Paths for the Development of Farmers' Cooperatives in Guangxi

Photo Album of Guangxi Rural Poverty Alleviation Pilot Project with the World Bank Loan

Compiled by Foreign Capital Project Development Center for Rural Revitalization of Guangxi Zhuang Autonomous Region

Guangxi Science & Technology Publishing House

Foreword

The Guangxi Rural Poverty Alleviation Pilot Project Financed by the World Bank（hereinafter referred to as "the World Bank-Financed Project" or "the Project"）is the first single-province poverty alleviation project financed by the World Bank in Guangxi. The Project has a total investment of about RMB 1.1 billion yuan，including RMB 731 million yuan from World Bank loans. The Project area includes Tiandong County，Pingguo City，Leye County，Tianlin County in Baise City，and Yizhou District in Hechi City，Donglan County，Bama Yao Autonomous County，Fengshan County，Du'an Yao Autonomous County and Dahua Yao Autonomous County in Hechi City，covering 141 administrative villages，including 127 poverty-stricken villages（currently the villages have been lifted out of poverty）in 72 townships and towns，with a population of 323,000. Among them，approximately 109,000 people were registered as poor（in 2017）. The Project，taking farmers' professional cooperatives as the primary carrier，aims to improve opportunities for increasing rural households' income by demonstrating value chain development models. The Project comprises four components〔Component 1：Improving Pro-Poor Value Chains；Component 2：Improving Public Infrastructure Construction and Enhancing Public Service Levels；Component 3：Enhancing Investments in Poor Areas；Component 4：Project Management，Monitoring and Evaluation（M&E），and Learning〕. By June 2024，the Project has supported the construction of 129 farmers' professional cooperatives in 10 counties（county-level cities and districts）of Baise and Hechi. In the process of assisting poverty alleviation and rural revitalization，the World Bank-Financed Project has innovatively accumulated experience in regional comprehensive development，full-industry chain creation，and whole-process monitoring and management for the development of farmers' cooperatives，which has achieved positive results.

In order to better summarize and showcase the outcomes of the Project，this photo album has been specially compiled by the Foreign Capital Project Development Center of Rural Revitalization of Guangxi Zhuang Autonomous Region. The photo album is divided into 3 chapters：project overview，project outcomes，and overviews of the Project in various counties（county-level cities and districts）. It displays the Project's implementation and outcome impacts（Please scan the QR code to watch more related videos），introducing the project background，management structure，construction content，experience and practices，and innovations. The goal of this photo album is to provide useful references and insights for the current work of rural revitalization.

Contents

Chapter I
Project Overview

Project Background and Overview

Guangxi Zhuang Autonomous Region, one of the five ethnic minority autonomous regions in China, has 12 native ethnic groups, including Zhuang, Han, Yao, Miao and Dong. Located in South China, it borders the Guangdong-Hong Kong-Macao Greater Bay Area and faces Southeast Asia. It is an important hub on the 21st Century Maritime Silk Road and holds a unique position in the overall pattern of China's Opening-up Strategy and Western Development Strategy. Following the launch of a new round of poverty alleviation and development in 2011, the rural poor population in Guangxi was reduced from 10.12 million in 2010 to 5.38 million by the end of 2014. Although poverty alleviation and development efforts achieved phased results, significant challenges, such as a large poverty-stricken rural area, a large number of poor people, and high levels of poverty, still existed. Thus, Guangxi remained one of China's primary provincial regions engaged in the battle against poverty.

To thoroughly implement the *Outline of China's Rural Poverty Alleviation and Development（2011-2020）* and achieve the grand objectives of winning the fight against poverty period and finishing building a moderately prosperous society in all respects at the same pace with the whole country by 2020, Guangxi took poverty alleviation as the top priority and the first livelihood project, and pooled the strength of all shareholders in this region to promote poverty alleviation. Under the guidance of the National Development and Reform Commission（NDRC）of People's Republic of China, the Ministry of Finance（MOF）of the People's Republic of China, and the National Rural Revitalization Administration（NRRA, formerly the State Council Leading Group Office of Poverty Alleviation and Development）, Guangxi cooperated with the World Bank to implement the Guangxi Rural Poverty Alleviation Pilot Project Financed by the World Bank（hereinafter referred to as "the World Bank-Financed Project" or "the Project"）. It employed a pilot approach to demonstrate value chain development models, increase rural residents' incomes, and foster inclusive and innovative development. The project period started on June 19, 2017, and will end on June 30, 2024. The World Bank-Financed Project has served China's Poverty Alleviation Strategy and conformed to the requirements of the World Bank's Country Partnership Strategy（FY 2013-2016）. The efforts to combine short-term support with long-term development measures and integrate rural households' self-development with increased interest bonding have effectively linked the consolidation and expansion of poverty alleviation achievements and rural revitalization in Guangxi.

Total Project Investment

★ The total investment of the Project is RMB **1.1** billion yuan, including USD **0.1** billion of World Bank loans and RMB **0.442** billion yuan of domestic matching funds.

¥ Domestic matching funds

RMB **0.442** billion yuan

¥ Loans from the World Bank

USD **0.1** billion

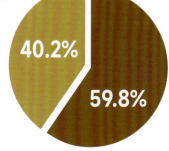

40.2%

59.8%

Areas Covered by the Project

★ The Project has benefited **141** administrative villages of **72** townships and towns in **10** counties（county-level cities and districts）of Guangxi, including **127** poverty-stricken villages（currently the villages have been lifted out of poverty）.

About **109,000** people registered as poor （in 2017）

Covering a population of **323,000**

Project Milestones and Management Organization Structure

1. Project Milestones

November 24-28，2014	The World Bank sent a project pre-identification mission to Guangxi and the Guangxi Foreign Capital Poverty Reduction Project Management Center sent staff to Tiandong and Du'an counties for field visits.
April 2015	The World Bank's project identification mission held discussions with authorities of Guangxi Zhuang Autonomous Region，including its development and reform commission，finance department，and poverty alleviation office，and conducted field visits to Leye and Donglan Counties.
October 2015	The World Bank's project preparation mission paid field visits to Fengshan County，Bama Yao Autonomous County and Pingguo County. During this period，they conducted in-depth discussions with Guangxi on project design parameters and project implementation and funding plans.
March 21-25 & April 18-29，2016	The World Bank's pre-appraisal mission discussed project documents and activity plans with Guangxi's authorities. During this period，a field visit was paid to Bama Yao Autonomous County.
June 20-July 1，2016	The World Bank's appraisal mission discussed project result framework indicators with the Guangxi Foreign Capital Poverty Reduction Project Management Center. During this period，field visits were paid to Tianlin and Tiandong counties and county-level feasibility study reports were reviewed.
November 30，2016	The World Bank issued the Project Appraisal Document.
February 27，2017	The Ministry of Finance of the People's Republic of China and the World Bank signed the *Loan Agreement Between the People's Republic of China and the International Bank for Reconstruction and Development* (*Guangxi Rural Poverty Alleviation Pilot Project in Poverty-Stricken Areas*)，and the People's Government of Guangxi Zhuang Autonomous Region and the World Bank signed the *Project Agreement Between the People's Republic of China and the International Bank for Reconstruction and Development* (*Guangxi Rural Poverty Alleviation Pilot Project in Poverty-stricken Areas*) (hereinafter referred to as "the *Project Agreement*").
April 7，2017	The kick-off meeting of the World Bank-Financed Project was held in Pingguo County. Huang Ribo，then Vice Chairman of the People's Government of Guangxi Zhuang Autonomous Region，and Zoubida Kherous Allaoua，Deputy Director for China，Mongolia and Korea from the World Bank，attended the meeting and delivered speeches. Ms. Zoubida Kherous Allaoua highly affirmed the efforts of Guangxi and said in her speech，"The management team and PMO at the autonomous region level are very capable. We hope that the high-capacity operation mode of the Guangxi RPMO can be introduced into the project management efforts of other provinces in China."
May 2017	The Poverty Alleviation and Development Office of Guangxi Zhuang Autonomous Region held the 2017 procurement and cooperative management training course for the World Bank-Financed Project.
June 19，2017	The *Project Agreement* came into effect.
July 2017	The World Bank's technical mission went to Guangxi to guide the Project's implementation and review and discuss the Project's arrangements in areas such as Business Incubation Centers and the Matching Grant for Enterprises. During this period，field visits were paid to Tianlin County，Tiandong County，Du'an Yao Autonomous County and Yizhou District of Hechi City to inspect the progress of the Project.
September 2017	Approved by the People's Government of Guangxi Zhuang Autonomous Region，an inter-departmental joint meeting mechanism for the World Bank-Financed Project was established. The Poverty Alleviation and Development Office of Guangxi Zhuang Autonomous Region established the Regional Project Management Office for the World Bank-Financed Project (hereinafter referred to as "RPMO"). RPMO and the Department of Finance of Guangxi Zhuang Autonomous Region jointly held the 2017 financial management，withdrawal and reimbursement training course for the World Bank-Financed Project.

October 2017	*The Implementation Management Manual of Guangxi Rural Poverty Alleviation Pilot Project Financed by the World Bank* was issued.
November 19-30，2017	The First Implementation Support Mission of the World Bank went to Guangxi for the Project's implementation. During this period，field visits were paid to Dahua Yao Autonomous County，Donglan County，and Pingguo County to inspect the progress of the Project.
May 28-June 2，2018	The Second Implementation Support Mission of the World Bank went to Guangxi for the Project's implementation. During this period，field visits were paid to Tiandong County and Du'an Yao Autonomous County to inspect the progress of the Project.
October 2018	RPMO held the field observation，exchange and training course for the World Bank-Financed Project and training courses on project management information system and financial and procurement management in Pingguo County.
November 26-December 9，2018	The Third Implementation Support Mission of the World Bank went to Guangxi for the Project's implementation. During this period，field visits were paid to Bama Yao Autonomous County，Fengshan County and Tianlin County to inspect the progress of the Project.
January 2019	RPMO organized the 2018 financial inspection and research guidance for the Project and held special training sessions by experts from the Matching Grant for Enterprises Review Expert Database.
March 2019	RPMO held the cooperative training and capacity building training course for the World Bank-Financed Project.
June 24-July 5，2019	The Fourth Implementation Support Mission of the World Bank went to Guangxi for the Project's implementation. During this period，field visits were paid to Dahua Yao Autonomous County，Donglan County and Fengshan County to inspect the progress of the Project.
July 2019	RPMO organized the financial inspection and research guidance for the Project for the first half of 2019.
October 2019	RPMO held the management training course for the World Bank-Financed Project.
November 4-19，2019	The Fifth Implementation Support Mission of the World Bank went to Guangxi for the Project's implementation. During this period，field visits were paid to Pingguo County，Tiandong County，Yizhou District of Hechi City and Dahua Yao Autonomous County to inspect the progress of the Project.
January 2020	RPMO held the 2020 project training course and organized the 2019 financial inspection，third-party monitoring and research guidance for the Project.
May 11-22，2020	Affected by the COVID-19 pandemic，the World Bank's Sixth Implementation Support Mission worked online and entrusted RPMO to pay field visits to Dahua Yao Autonomous County，Donglan County，and Tiandong County in an effort to inspect the Project.
July 2020	RPMO organized the financial inspection，third-party monitoring and research guidance for the Project for the first half of 2020.
October 2020	RPMO conducted the mid-term adjustment of the Project.
October 19-November 1，2020	The Seventh Implementation Support Mission of the World Bank went to Guangxi for the implementation and mid-term inspection of the Project. During this period，field visits were paid to Pingguo City，Dahua Yao Autonomous County，Bama Yao Autonomous County and Donglan County to inspect the progress of the Project.
January 2021	RPMO held the 2021 project training course and organized the 2020 financial inspection，third-party monitoring and research guidance for the Project.
June 21-26，2021	The Eighth Implementation Support Mission of the World Bank went to Guangxi for the Project's implementation. During this period，field visits were paid to Leye and Fengshan counties to inspect the progress of the Project.

July 2021	RPMO organized the financial inspection, third-party monitoring and research guidance for the Project for the first half of 2021.
December 13-17, 2021	The Ninth Implementation Support Mission of the World Bank went to Guangxi for the Project's implementation. During this period, a field visit was paid to Yizhou District of Hechi City to inspect the progress of the Project.
January 2022	RPMO held the 2022 project training course and organized the 2021 financial inspection, third-party monitoring and research guidance for the Project.
June 20-23, 2022	Affected by the COVID-19 pandemic, the World Bank's Tenth Implementation Support Mission facilitated the Project's implementation online.
July 2022	RPMO organized the financial inspection, third-party monitoring and research guidance for the Project for the first half of 2022.
September 2022	An onsite promotion meeting on the World Bank-Financed Project was held in Yizhou District, Hechi City.
December 20-23, 2022	Affected by the COVID-19 pandemic, the World Bank's Eleventh Implementation Support Mission facilitated the Project's implementation online.
January 2023	RPMO held the 2023 project training course and organized the 2022 financial inspection, third-party monitoring and research guidance for the Project.
April 2023	RPMO held a series of seminars on consulting services for Business Incubation Centers.
June 12-16, 2023	The Twelfth Implementation Support Mission of the World Bank went to Guangxi for the Project's implementation. During this period, field visits were paid to Yizhou District of Hechi City and Tiandong County to inspect the progress of the Project.
July 2023	RPMO organized the financial inspection, third-party monitoring and research guidance for the Project for the first half of 2023.
November 2023	The World Bank-financed Guangxi Rural Poverty Alleviation Pilot Demonstration Project implemented by related governmental institutions in Yizhou District, Hechi City, entitled "Full-process Support for the Sericulture Industry Value Chain, Assistance for Sericulturists to Sustainably Increase Income and Become Rich", was rated as the best poverty reduction case in the Fourth Call of Global Solicitation on Best Poverty Reduction Practices.
December 4-8, 2023	The Thirteenth Implementation Support Mission of the World Bank went to Guangxi for the Project's implementation. During this period, field visits were paid to Tianlin County and Du'an Yao Autonomous County to inspect the progress of the Project.
December 2023-January 2024	RPMO organized the 2023 financial inspection, third-party monitoring and research guidance for the Project.
February 2024	RPMO held the 2024 project training course.
April 2024	The "Lively Spring in Beautiful Du'an" —2024 Direct Sales Activity of Agricultural and Specialty Products from Farmers' Professional Cooperatives and SMEs Supported by the World Bank-Financed Project was held in Shenzhen City, Guangdong Province.
May 13-17, 2024	The Fourteenth Implementation Support Mission/Implementation Completion Mission of the World Bank went to Guangxi for work. During this period, field research on Donglan County was conducted.
June 30, 2024	This is the loan closing date of the Project.

Developments

In April, a training session was carried out on the management and design of the World Bank-Financed Project.

In March, the World Bank's pre-appraisal mission（Phase Ⅰ）conducted an investigation, with the participation of relevant persons in charge from the RPMO and Project Management Offices of Baise City and Hechi City.

2015

2016

In January, a training course was held on the preparation of the World Bank-Financed Project investment plan and the establishment（reconstruction）of cooperatives.

In April, the World Bank's pre-appraisal mission （Phase Ⅱ）held a symposium.

In November, representatives from the People's Government of Guangxi Zhuang Autonomous Region and the World Bank negotiated and signed a contract in Beijing.

2017

In April, Zoubida Kherous Allaoua (third from right), then Deputy Director for China, Mongolia and Korea from the World Bank, and his delegation paid a field visit to the Dragon Fruit Cooperative in Pingguo County.

In June, the World Bank's pre-appraisal mission paid a field visit to Tianlin County.

Organization and Implementation

On April 7, the kick-off meeting of the World Bank-Financed Project was held in Pingguo County. Huang Ribo, then Vice Chairman of the People's Government of Guangxi Zhuang Autonomous Region, and Zoubida Kherous Allaoua, then Deputy Director for China, Mongolia and Korea from the World Bank attended the meeting and delivered speeches.

On October 21, the RPMO held the first field observation and experience exchange and training course in Pingguo County.

2017   **2018** **2019**

In September, the 2017 Financial Management, Withdrawal and Reimbursement Training Course for the World Bank-Financed Project was held.

In November, the World Bank's First Implementation Support Mission visited Tianlin County for inspection and guidance. Josef Ernstberger, a Project Consultant of the World Bank, talked with staff from the Project Management Office of Tianlin County in front of the mango base.

In June, the World Bank's Fourth Implementation Support Mission visited Fengshan County for a feedback meeting.

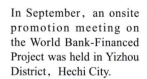

In October, the interim report meeting of the World Bank-Financed Project was held.

In September, Liu Kang (second from left), Deputy Director-General of the Department of Agriculture and Rural Affairs of Guangxi Zhuang Autonomous Region (then Chief Economist of the Rural Revitalization Administration of Guangxi Zhuang Autonomous Region), visited cooperatives in Pingguo city for field research.

On May 10, the video scheduling meeting of the World Bank-Financed Project was held.

2020　　**2021**　　**2022**

In October, the RPMO held a seminar on the mid-term adjustment of the World Bank-Financed Project.

In September, an onsite promotion meeting on the World Bank-Financed Project was held in Yizhou District, Hechi City.

In April, the RPMO held a series of seminars on consulting services for Business Incubation Centers.

In June, the World Bank's Twelfth Implementation Support Mission visited Fuxinyuan Planting and Breeding Farmers' Professional Cooperative in Yizhou District, Hechi City, Guangxi for field research. The photo shows Ladisy Komba Chengula (second from right), a Project Team Leader of the World Bank, inspecting the cooperative's agricultural product perfume lemon.

2023

In April, the Direct Sales Activity of Agricultural and Specialty Products from Farmers' Professional Cooperatives and SMEs Supported by the World Bank-Financed Project was held in the Three Streets and Two Alleys of Nanning City.

In June, the World Bank's Twelfth Implementation Support Mission visited Guangxi Tiandong Modern Agriculture Investment Co., Ltd. to inspect the production of dried mango.

In December, the launch meeting of the World Bank's Thirteenth Implementation Support Mission was held.

In February, a training course was carried out on the management of the World Bank-Financed Project.

2024

In December, the World Bank's Thirteenth Implementation Support Mission visited Tianlin Business Incubation Center for field research.

In April, the "Lively Spring in Beautiful Du'an" —2024 Direct Sales Activity of Agricultural and Specialty Products from Farmers' Professional Cooperatives and SMEs Supported by the World Bank-Financed Project was held in Shenzhen City, Guangdong Province.

2. Project Management Organization Structure

As per the demand for project organization, implementation and management, a three-tiered project management organization structure at the autonomous region, city, and county levels has been established. Guangxi Zhuang Autonomous Region has established a project inter-departmental joint meeting mechanism, beneath which the RPMO is set as a part of the Rural Revitalization Administration of Guangxi Zhuang Autonomous Region （formerly the Poverty Alleviation and Development Office of Guangxi Zhuang Autonomous Region）. The Foreign Capital Project Development Center, Rural Revitalization Administration of Guangxi Zhuang Autonomous Region （formerly Guangxi Foreign Capital Poverty Reduction Project Management Center） is responsible for implementing and managing the Project. Municipal-level PMOs are established as a part of the rural revitalization bureaus of cities where the Project is implemented. They are responsible for managing the specific city-level project affairs and supervising, guiding, and inspecting the Project's implementation in the project counties within their jurisdictions. In the project counties, leading groups and technical （expert advisory） committees are established to lead, coordinate, and provide technical support for the Project. County PMOs are established under the county-level rural revitalization bureaus and they are responsible for organizing, implementing and managing the Project.

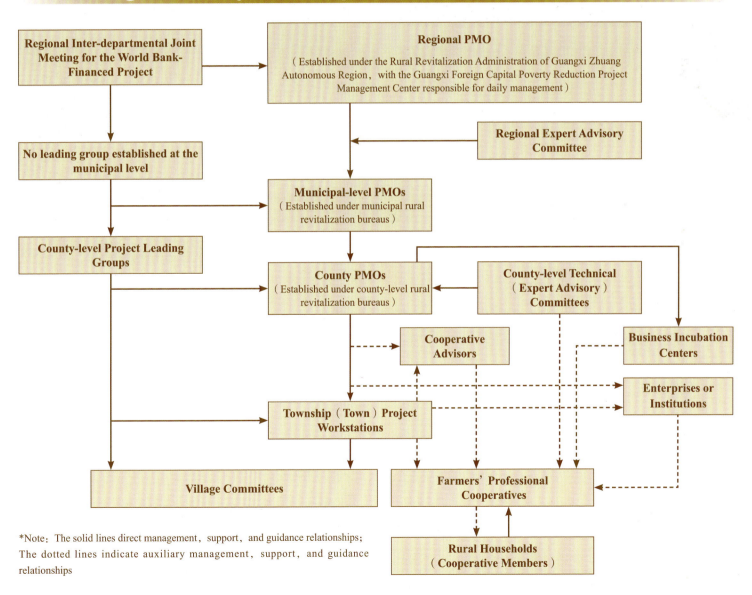

Figure of Project Management Organization Structure

*Note：The solid lines direct management, support, and guidance relationships；
The dotted lines indicate auxiliary management, support, and guidance relationships

Chapter Ⅱ
Project Outcomes

Project Development Results

Component 1： Improving Pro-Poor Value Chains

This component aims to address market failures in the development of agricultural and non-agricultural rural value chains and key industries with a particular focus on increasing the value of economic activities of targeted farmers' cooperatives. Component 1 has the following two subcomponents： Cooperative Development Fund and Matching Grant for Enterprises.

Participatory Planning and Cooperative Establishment Meeting for the Rural Poverty Alleviation Pilot Project in Pingliu Village， Suolue Township Financed by the World Bank in April 2016

1. Cooperative Development Fund

The Cooperative Development Fund（CDF）provides grant financing to new or existing cooperatives. The cooperatives used the CDF to invest primarily in fixed value-adding production， provide corresponding supporting facilities， small-scale infrastructure， goods， and technical support facilities， and carry out cooperative capacity building. Attention has been paid to strengthening the organizational structures and management capabilities of the cooperatives. Specific measures have been taken to ensure the active participation of women in cooperative activities as individual members. The project cooperatives develop their cooperative investment plans with the help of technical experts， agro-enterprises， and county-level governmental departments. After these investment plans are evaluated and approved by the RPMO and County PMOs， the cooperatives should be responsible for implementing the plans and developing value chains.

In November 2017， experts of the World Bank's First Implementation Support Mission organized a review meeting on cooperative investment plans in Nanning

Mango Harvest of Tiandong Xiangzhou Lianqiang Planting and Breeding Farmers' Professional Cooperative

Black goats raised by Guangxi Pingguo Ruiyan Breeding Farmers' Professional Cooperative

Farm of Leye Sensen Ecological Cattle Breeding Specialized Cooperative

Members of Tianlin Xintai Planting and Breeding Specialized Cooperative Pressing Oil

Sericulture Base at Hechi Yizhou Gaoshou Silkworm Rearing Professional Cooperative

Harvest of Donglan Camellia Oleifera at Jiangdong Camellia Oleifera Farmers' Professional Cooperative

Fengshan Langli Hongxiang Breeding Professional Cooperative Making Chili Sauce with Camellia Oil

Cattle Farm of Du'an Shengxing Ecological Breeding Professional Cooperative

Dividend Distribution at Dahua Yantan Xianwang Farmers' Professional Cooperative

Member Meeting of Bama Jingfeng Planting and Breeding Farmers' Professional Cooperative

2. Matching Grant for Enterprises

The MG provides matching grants of up to 30% of the total investment in the Project Investment Plan for independent qualified enterprises or enterprises that have established partnerships with farmer cooperatives. After transparent evaluation and selection of outstanding competitors, the MG has supported enterprises to strengthen interest bonding and sharing with cooperatives and rural households through investment activities. While the demonstration and leading role of these enterprises is fully leveraged, the ownership has been ensured and the public welfare feature of private investment activities has been increased.

The Project involves 12 enterprises, with grants from the World Bank amounting to RMB

65.5906 million yuan

and self-raised funds amounting to RMB

179.8480 million yuan

Driving the development of **336** associated cooperatives and village collectives

About **100,000** rural households

Developing industries with local characteristics

Products Produced by the Matching Grant Beneficiary Guangxi Xianyou Agricultural Development Co., Ltd.

Products Produced by the Matching Grant Beneficiary Guangxi Tianlin County Xinfuyuan Camellia Oil Development Co., Ltd.

Exhibition Hall of the Kanghui Beef Cattle Breeding Base of the Matching Grant Beneficiary Guangxi Leye Huadong Investment Co., Ltd.

Production Workshop of the Matching Grant Beneficiary Guangxi Jialian Silk Co., Ltd.

Products Produced by the Matching Grant Beneficiary Guangxi Wehand-Bio Pharmaceutical Co., Ltd.

Production Workshop of the Matching Grant Beneficiary Guangxi Donglan Huashen Silk Co., Ltd.

Smart Mobile Fruiting Greenhouse of the Matching Grant Beneficiary Guangxi Donglan Guilong Ecological Agriculture Technology Co., Ltd.

Exhibits at the Exhibition Hall of the Matching Grant Beneficiary Guangxi Hefeng Pharmaceutical Co., Ltd.

Bama Ecological Beef Cattle Industry Core Demonstration Area of the Matching Grant Beneficiary Guangxi Bama Babaili Agriculture Co., Ltd.

Slaughter Workshop of the Matching Grant Beneficiary Guangxi Bama Xiaogu Chicken Breeding Co., Ltd.

Planting Base of the Matching Grant Beneficiary Guangxi Fengshan Jiahong Seedling Co., Ltd.

Chicken Coop Built by Matching Grant Beneficiary Guangxi Dahua Guitong Agriculture and Forestry Development Co., Ltd.

Component 2: Improving Public Infrastructure Construction and Enhancing Public Service Levels

This component can support the construction of public infrastructure and improvement of public service levels related to the value chain/key industry development under Component 1. It includes two subcomponents: rural infrastructure construction and industrial chain risk management.

1. Rural Infrastructure Construction

This subcomponent focuses on the development of cooperatives and industries. Support has been provided to improve rural infrastructure construction, enhance public service levels, and resolve issues related to water and electricity usage for living and production and challenges in transporting agricultural products out.

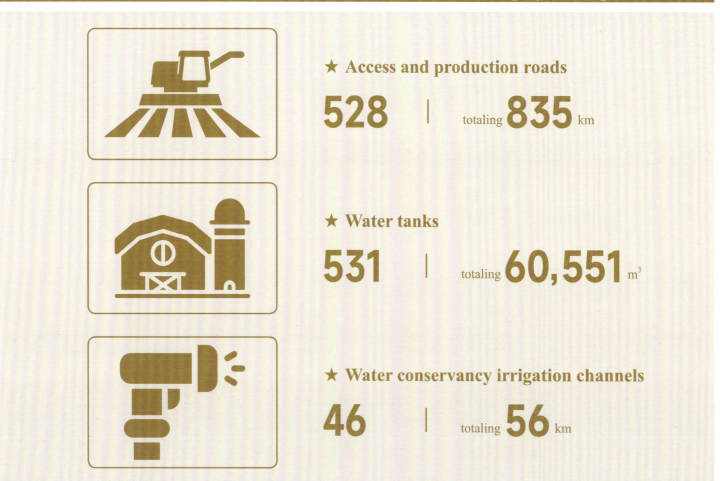

By the end of 2023, various facilities had been built in 139 project villages.

★ **Access and production roads**

528 | totaling **835** km

★ **Water tanks**

531 | totaling **60,551** m³

★ **Water conservancy irrigation channels**

46 | totaling **56** km

Gravel Road Construction Project for Camellia Oleifera Industrial Base in Nadu Village，Jiuzhou Town，Tianlin County

Industrial Road Hardening Project for Hechi City Yuanyuan Planting and Breeding Professional Cooperative Supported by World Bank Matching Funds

The Water Storage Tanks of Fengshan Gengsha Shunfa Farmers' Professional Cooperative During Construction（Left）and After Construction（Right）

The Plant of Fengshan County Hesheng Agricultural and Sideline Product Processing Professional Cooperative During Construction（Left）and After Construction（Right）

2. Industrial Chain Risk Management

This subcomponent aims to support project counties to develop value chains and formulate and implement industry-level comprehensive risk assessment and risk mitigation plans that consider production，market，financial，and other risks.

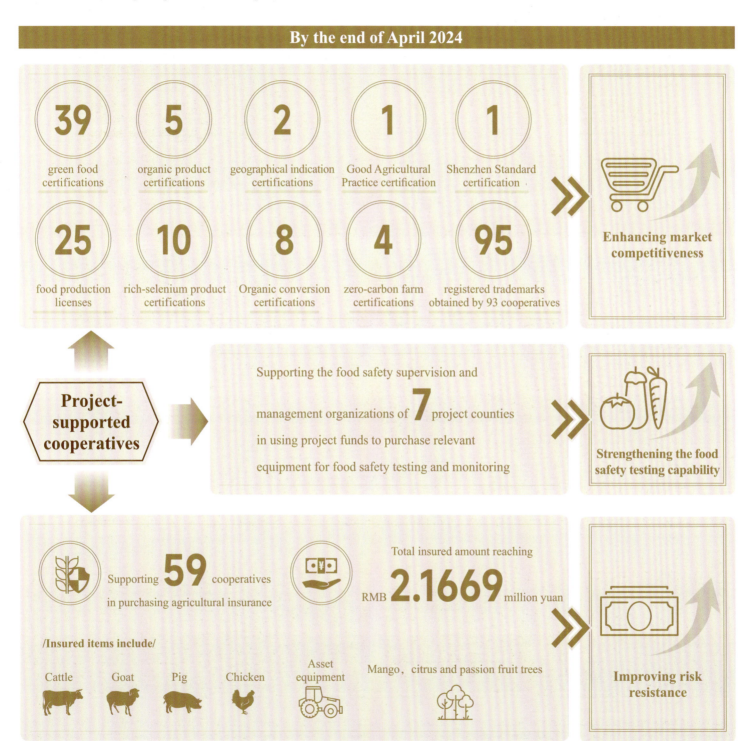

By the end of April 2024

39 green food certifications

5 organic product certifications

2 geographical indication certifications

1 Good Agricultural Practice certification

1 Shenzhen Standard certification

25 food production licenses

10 rich-selenium product certifications

8 Organic conversion certifications

4 zero-carbon farm certifications

95 registered trademarks obtained by 93 cooperatives

Enhancing market competitiveness

Project-supported cooperatives

Supporting the food safety supervision and management organizations of **7** project counties in using project funds to purchase relevant equipment for food safety testing and monitoring

Strengthening the food safety testing capability

Supporting **59** cooperatives in purchasing agricultural insurance

Total insured amount reaching RMB **2.1669** million yuan

/Insured items include/

Cattle Goat Pig Chicken Asset equipment Mango，citrus and passion fruit trees

Improving risk resistance

21

Green Food Certificate

Certificate of Se-rich Agricultural Products

Staff of the Rural Revitalization Research Institute of Bama Yao Autonomous County Conducting Food Safety Testing

Camellia Oil Production at Fengshan Native Camellia Oil Planting Professional Cooperative

Component 3：Enhancing Investments in Poor Areas

This component has improved and facilitated investments in rural areas by existing and new micro-entrepreneurs and business entities such as small and medium-sized enterprises（SMEs）, migrant returnees, or cooperatives.

1. Business Incubation Centers

This subcomponent aims to support the establishment of one business incubation center in each county. Targeted at serving county-level economic development, these centers are responsible for providing a range of regional specialized consultation services for small and medium-sized enterprises, farmers' professional cooperatives, returning entrepreneurs, and entrepreneurial leaders. Such services include technical training, legal aid, financial support, expert advice, and marketing. In addition, professional service platforms, such as websites, applications, and WeChat official accounts for World Bank-financed business service centers were established to more effectively address users' needs and pain points.

Business Incubation Center of Du'an Yao Autonomous County

Activities of Business Incubation Centers Supported by the World Bank-Financed Project

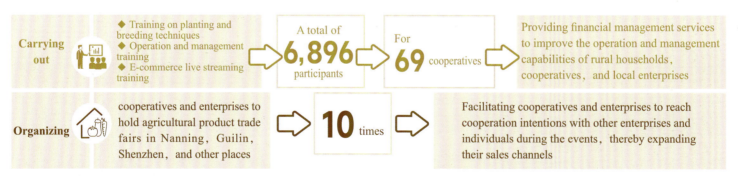

Carrying out
◆ Training on planting and breeding techniques
◆ Operation and management training
◆ E-commerce live streaming training

A total of **6,896** participants

For **69** cooperatives

Providing financial management services to improve the operation and management capabilities of rural households, cooperatives, and local enterprises

Organizing cooperatives and enterprises to hold agricultural product trade fairs in Nanning, Guilin, Shenzhen, and other places

10 times

Facilitating cooperatives and enterprises to reach cooperation intentions with other enterprises and individuals during the events, thereby expanding their sales channels

Pictures of the World Bank Regional Projects—2023 Special Agricultural Products Exhibition from Ten Counties（County-level Cities）

2.Improving Access to Financing

This subcomponent supports cooperation between counties and local financial institutions to establish a comprehensive credit rating system for rural households and cooperatives and facilitate rural asset appraisal. The validation and evaluation of rural asset rights allowed individual households and cooperatives to obtain loans from designated finance institutions.

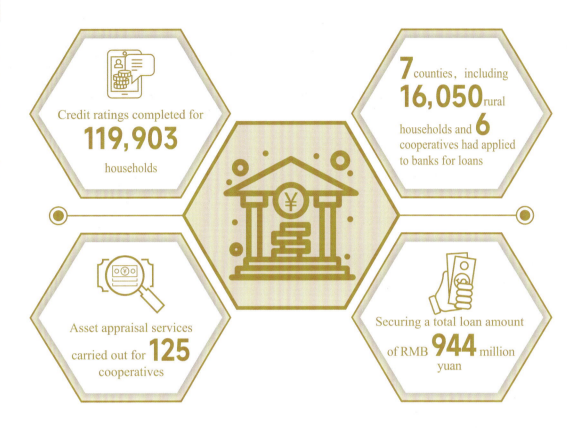

By the end of April 2024

Credit ratings completed for **119,903** households

7 counties, including **16,050** rural households and **6** cooperatives had applied to banks for loans

Asset appraisal services carried out for **125** cooperatives

Securing a total loan amount of RMB **944** million yuan

Asset Appraisal Services

Component 4: Project Management, Monitoring and Evaluation, and Learning

This component aims to strengthen and improve the administrative and technical capacity of the staff of the PMOs at the autonomous region, city, and county levels. It includes establishing a monitoring and evaluation (M&E) and impact evaluation system and introducing an external professional monitoring agency. This component also supports daily supervision, progress monitoring, completion acceptance, and supervision and monitoring of safeguards compliance and enables learning from pilot activities.

By the end of 2023, the RPMO and County PMOs had held a total of 143 training sessions with 7,565 participants and cumulatively organized 52 study tours with a total of 892 participants to regions such as Guizhou, Yunnan, Hunan, Fujian, Gansu, and Zhejiang. These tours were aimed at learning the experience and practices of cooperative construction and sustainable operation from the advanced regions.

2023 Training Course for the World Bank-Financed Project

A Study Tour to Leye County to Investigate the Role of the World Bank-Financed Project in Enhancing Cooperatives' Capacity Building

A Study Tour to Guizhou by the Project Management Office of Du'an Yao Autonomous County

Visiting Jiangsu Province to Hold the 2023 Training Course on Rural Revitalization and Agricultural Industry Development for the World Bank-Financed Project

25

Project Experience，Practices，and Innovations

Regarding industries as the focus and farmers' cooperatives as the primary carrier，the World Bank-Financed Project has persisted in finding favorable solutions to five issues and exploring new mechanisms and models for rural industrial development in areas that have been lifted out of poverty. The Project supports the entire process of industrial chain development. The establishment of cooperatives by rural households has been organized through a participatory approach and the distance between cooperatives and markets has been shortened through e-commerce and other means. An incentive mechanism has been introduced to strengthen interest bonding between enterprises and cooperatives. With a few project funds，the Project has attracted the participation of more social capital in industrial development to improve and extend the industrial and value chains of rural areas，promote the sustainable development of industries in the project area，and ensure a sustainable increase in farmers' incomes.

I. How to Utilize Funds—Making an Objective-oriented Systemic Design

1. Defining the Project Objective

★ Project development objective

To increase income generation opportunities through demonstration of value chain development models in the project area.

3 core indicators

The number of project-supported cooperatives making a profit；the number of product certificates and brand names obtained under the Project；the number of cooperative members.

4 intermediate results

（1）Improvement of Pro-Poor Value Chains
（2）Improving Public Infrastructure and Services
（3）Enhancing Investments in Poor Areas
（4）Project Management，M&E，and Learning

10 specific indicators

（1）The number of cooperatives that have received Cooperative Development Fund（cumulative）；
（2）Average cooperative management effectiveness（METT）score；
（3）The number of cooperative members who adopt innovative marketing practices；
（4）Customers satisfied with the rural infrastructure services provided by the Project；
（5）The number of value chains for which risk management plans were developed；
（6）Project management improvement actions triggered by grievances/complaints；
（7）Customers satisfied with the services provided by Business Incubation Center；
（8）The number of households in project areas covered by credit rating（cumulative）；
（9）Implementation of thematic seminars and meetings；
（10）The number of project-related publications produced.

2. Allocating Funds Based on the Objective

Project funds were allocated based on project objectives. Funds for each component were allocated based on their significance and contribution to the objectives.

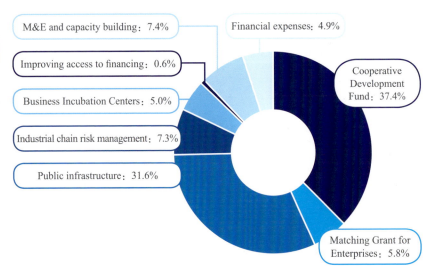

- M&E and capacity building：7.4%
- Financial expenses：4.9%
- Improving access to financing：0.6%
- Business Incubation Centers：5.0%
- Cooperative Development Fund：37.4%
- Industrial chain risk management：7.3%
- Public infrastructure：31.6%
- Matching Grant for Enterprises：5.8%

3. Annually Designing Project Plans

During the project period of six years, annual project plans have been formulated every year and fine-tuned according to the Project's implementation.

In August 2022, RPMO organized project management personnel from Baise City, Hechi City and 10 project counties (county-level cities and districts) to study and discuss the implementation of the annual project plans and adjustment arrangements.

4. Improving the Informatization of Project Fund Management

Project Management Information System (PROMIS) were utilized to manage fund operations, withdrawals, and expense reimbursement.

Interface of the Project Management Information System (PROMIS)

27

II. How to Act—Using a Regulation-oriented Approach to Conduct the Refined Management of the Entire Process of Project Implementation

1. Issuing Detailed Guidance Documents

RPMO has organized the preparation of a suite of documents, including the *Project Operation Manual*, *Procurement Management Manual*, *Financial Management Manual*, *Operation Guide for Farmers' Professional Cooperatives*, *Operation Guide for Business Incubation Centers*, and *Administrative Measures for the Matching Grant for Enterprises Subcomponent*. These documents have provided guidance for the standardized management and implementation of the Project.

2. Conducting Ex-ante Reviews of Project Plans

A review mechanism for project investment plans (implementation plans) has been established. Only the reviewed projects can be implemented. For example, for the Matching Grant for Enterprises (MG) subcomponent, a procedure titled "Two Reviews, One Examination, and One Announcement" has been implemented for strict admission and management.

"Two Reviews" refers to the process where two rounds of review should be conducted for the project investment plans submitted by qualified enterprises in the prescribed format. The first round of review involves expert review and field verification organized by County PMOs. The investment plans should be submitted to county governments for approval after passing the reviews of expert groups. The second round of review involves expert review and field verification organized by RPMO. Expert groups should grade these investment plans based on factors such as the performance of benefiting farmers and helping them develop, innovation, potential for added value generation, technical and financial viability, sustainability, and environmental impact.

"One Examination" refers to the process where RPMO submits the project investment plans passing the two rounds of review to the World Bank for examination.

"One Announcement" signifies that after the World Bank project team has reviewed the project investment plans, the list of enterprises proposed to be supported and the funds allocated accordingly should be disclosed online for seven days.

Enterprises can only receive grants after successfully going through the "Two Reviews, One Examination, and One Announcement" procedure.

Announcement on the List of Enterprises Proposed to be Supported by the MG Subcomponent of the World Bank–Financed Project and Relevant Funds

Review Meeting on Project Investment Plans for the Matching Grant for Enterprises

RPMO Organizing Experts to Conduct A Field Verification to Guangxi Donglan Huashen Silk Co., Ltd., the Enterprise Applying for the MG

3. Signing Project Implementation Agreements

After each subcomponent's investment plan（implementation plan）is revised according to opinions and suggestions of expert groups, implementing entities（cooperatives, enterprises, relevant institutions, etc.）have entered into an implementation agreement with County PMOs. This agreement specifies the liability clauses related to the mechanism of benefiting farmers and helping them develop and pledges specific quantitative indicators for leading the development of registered poor households. Additionally, it puts forward the following requirements, including organizing the Project's implementation, procurement, and training as per the *Project Operations Manual*; using earmarked funds only for their designated purposes, conducting independent accounting for a dedicated account, designating special personnel for management, and auditing and disbursing the funds as per the system of accounting report.

4. Strengthening Internal Management and External Monitoring

Comprehensive management and monitoring have been conducted during the entire process of the Project to ensure that progress is visible, issues are controllable, and objectives are achievable. For one thing, project oversight has been strengthened using a three-pronged approach, in which County PMOs are responsible for specific management and supervision, RPMO is responsible for routine guidance and inspection, and the Audit Office of Guangxi Zhuang Autonomous Region is responsible for regular project audits. For another, independent third-party institutions, in accordance with project implementation agreements and investment plans, have conducted regular on-site surveys and inspections in areas such as the progress and quality of project implementation, industrial development scale, value-adding revenue from industrial chains, establishment and execution of interest bonding mechanisms, coverage of and leadership over households lifted out of poverty and monitored households, as well as technical support. These institutions have then published evaluation reports and provided feedback to PMOs at both the autonomous region and county levels to rectify any shortcomings.

In September 2022, Liu Kang, Deputy Director-General of the Department of Agriculture and Rural Affairs of Guangxi Zhuang Autonomous Region（then Chief Economist of the Rural Revitalization Administration of Guangxi Zhuang Autonomous Region）, paid field research on Hechi Yizhou Wangteng Ecological Agriculture Development Professional Cooperative.

Nanning Normal University Conducting the Third-party Monitoring and Evaluation of the World Bank-Financed Project

RPMO Organizing the Financial Inspection of the Project for the First Half of 2022

RPMO Organizing the Financial Inspection of the Project for the First Half of 2023

5. Building a Specialized Talent Team

First, a specialized consulting team has been introduced to provide PMOs and cooperatives with technical guidance in areas such as industrial development, cooperative management, finance, procurement, environment and social security.

Second, a project database of experts specializing in agricultural economy, marketing, food safety, law, financing, and other disciplines has been established. Through expert reviews, the investment plans of enterprises and cooperatives have been properly managed to avoid blind and ineffective investments.

Third, support has been given to cultivate self-owned talent. Each cooperative has been staffed with a special instructor, who is responsible for organizing various kinds of training for project personnel and cooperative members.

| Project management training and procurement and financial management training **69** sessions | Training on planting and breeding techniques **31** sessions | Operation and management training **31** sessions | E-commerce live-streaming training **12** sessions | A total of **7,565** participants |

Rural Revitalization and Agricultural Industrial Development Training Course (Second Semester) of the World Bank Financed Project

Fengshan County Hesheng Agricultural and Sideline Product Processing Professional Cooperative Holding Training on Sweet Potato Planting Techniques

Legal Risk Prevention and Control Consultation for Guangxi Tiandong Zihe Planting and Breeding Farmers' Professional Cooperative

Mango Experts from Tiandong County Conducting Training on Mango Management Techniques in the Mango Base

III. How to Sell Products—Adopting a Market-oriented Approach to Improve the Entire Industrial Chain

1. Addressing Planting and Breeding Risks

First，epidemic prevention and control have been carried out. In addition to regular planting and breeding technology training，the Project has also supported counties（county-level cities and districts）to provide consulting services on animal disease prevention and control. Cooperatives can fully utilize experts' professional advantages to solve the problems they have encountered. Second，insurance has been purchased. The cooperatives have used project funds to purchase animal and plant insurance，thereby reducing their planting and breeding risks.

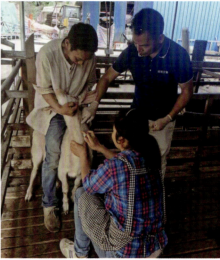

Disease Prevention and Control of Livestock and Poultry

Members and Chairman of Guangxi Dahua Qibainong Kangli Breeding Professional Cooperative Vaccinating Chickens in Chicken Coop

Insurance Policy for Chicken

Commercial Insurance Policy for Orah Mandarin

Commercial Insurance Policy for Finishing Pigs

2. Increasing the Added Value of Products

With the support of the World Bank-Financed Project，the industrial chains have been extended and the value chains have been improved. Cooperatives have been incentivized to engage in the whole process of agricultural product production，including planting，breeding，harvesting，and processing. Support has also been given to trademark registration，green food certification，organic product certification，and geographical indication certification to broaden the sales channels of products and increase their market competitiveness.

By the end of April 2024

✓ **25** cooperatives had obtained food production licenses

✓ **93** cooperatives had obtained registered trademarks

✓ A total of **70** certifications in areas such as green food，organic products and geographical indications had been obtained.

Chili Sauce with Camellia Oil with a Registered Trademark Produced by Fengshan Langli Hongxiang Breeding Professional Cooperative

Green Food Certification of Camellia Oil Produced by Leye Qiangmin Camellia Oil Planting Farmers' Professional Cooperative

Products of Bama Furao Oil Tea Farmers' Professional Cooperative Obtained Organic Product Certification

Registered Trademark Obtained by Fengshan Langli Hongxiang Breeding Professional Cooperative

3. Improving Industrial Competitiveness

During the entire process of the Project, project funds have been used to support local advantageous and characteristic industries such as Yizhou's silkworm, Tiandong's mango, and Tianlin's camellia oil. These funds have contributed to enhancing the deep processing capacity of a group of leading enterprises, broadening enterprises' marketing channels, increasing the comprehensive income of the industrial chains, and bringing benefits to cooperatives and rural households. Twelve enterprises have cumulatively received project grants amounting to RMB 65.5906 million yuan, while the enterprises themselves have raised investment funds totaling RMB 179.8480 million yuan. These funds have incentivized the development of local characteristic industries, involving 336 associated cooperatives and village collectives and approximately 100, 000 rural households.

Dyeing Workshop of Guangxi Jialian Silk Co., Ltd.

Kiwifruit Harvest of Guangxi Leye Mixiang Fruit Professional Cooperative

Mango Deep Processing Workshop of Guangxi Xianyou Agricultural Development Co., Ltd.

4. Aiding Sales Growth Through Multiple Channels

Project funds have been used to establish applications, video accounts, and WeChat official accounts customized for cooperatives and county-level small and micro-sized enterprises, cultivate e-commerce livestreamers for cooperatives, and build online sales channels. Additionally, Project funds have been used to conduct e-commerce training, build livestreaming venues in Business Incubation Centers, and organize product trade fairs to aid the face-to-face communication and matchmaking between cooperatives and their customers like catering enterprises and chain convenience stores, and promote the achievement of sales intentions.

World Bank-Financed Project Business Service Center Official Website: http://www.gxshfh.cn/serviceHall

Video Account Page for World Bank-Financed Project Business Service Center

Wechat Account Page for World Bank-Financed Project Business Service Center

By the end of 2023

★ Counties（county-level cities and districts）had cumulatively hosted **12** e-commerce training

★ Established **204** accounts across platforms

★ Trained **529** trainees

★ Co-organized **612** livestreaming sessions

Approximately **6,817** orders of agricultural products had been sold, with a transaction volume of RMB **4.63** million yuan

A marketing matchmaking meeting supported by the World Bank-Financed Project was held in Nanning，attracting the participation of 36 project cooperatives and 60 catering and agricultural product sales enterprises in total. The production-marketing matchmaking model effectively shortened the sales process and thus，the local specialties of the cooperatives were sold directly to end consumers in Nanning.

From April 28 to May 1,2023，an Agricultural Product Marketing Matchmaking Meeting Supported by the World Bank-Financed Project Was Held by Du'an Yao Autonomous County in Three Streets and Two Alleys，Nanning.

IV. How to Distribute Benefits: Ensuring the Interests of Households Lifted Out of Poverty and the Vulnerable Women Group with a Focus on Cooperative Member

1. Preparing Clear Equity and Profit Distribution Plans

A single natural person member of a cooperative should be limited to holding not more than 30% of the cooperative members' total contributed capital. Minority shareholders' equity holdings should be capped at 40%. At the initiation phase, a cooperative is required to have at least 30 members, at least 20% of which should be members from households lifted out of poverty. During the project investment plan application phase, rigorous scrutiny of the profit distribution plan is required. 60% of the cooperative's surplus should be allocated for rebates based on members' transaction volumes, while the remaining 40% should be distributed according to equity. This approach has ensured that the majority of members are benefited.

2. Clarifying the Responsibility of Uniting Farmers and Helping Them Develop

The MG investment plans should clearly state the ways to benefit households lifted out of poverty and their quantitative indicators. Third-party professional organizations should regularly verify the completion of these plans to guarantee that both cooperatives and rural households participate in the enterprises' value-adding and income-increasing activities and receive a fair share of the profit.

Matching Grant Beneficiary Guangxi Tianlin County Xinfuyuan Camellia Oil Development Co., Ltd. Issuing Work Certificates to Employed Rural Households

Member Meeting of Fengshan Langli Hongxiang Professional Cooperative

Guangxi Wehand-Bio Pharmaceutical Co., Ltd. Purchasing Mulberry Twigs from Rural Households to Increase Their Income

3. Guaranteeing the Sustainability of Project Outcomes

There are 16,236 members in the project cooperatives, including 6,787 women, accounting for 42.1%, and 10,316 people who have been lifted out of poverty, accounting for 64%.

By the end of 2023

6,787 women
accounting for 42.1%

10,316 people lifted out of poverty, accounting for 64%

Total amount of dividends RMB **7.685** million yuan

The number of members benefiting from the Project (One person per household) **6,892**

The number of households lifted out of poverty **4,085**

16,236 members in the project cooperatives

129 cooperatives supported by the Project

Female Members of Dahua Yantan Xian-wang Farmers' Professional Cooperative Crushing Forage Grass

Fengshan Native Camellia Oil Planting Professional Cooperative Providing Employment Opportunities for Women

Members of Leye Qiangmin Camellia Oleifera Planting Farmers' Professional Cooperative Manually Shelling Camellia Seeds

Members of Dahua Donghuangling Farmers' Professional Cooperative Getting Their Dividends

V. How to Manage Assets — Clarifying the Responsibilities，Rights，and Obligations of All Parties with Property Rights as the Core

 ★ Assets formed through Matching Grant for Enterprises（MG）investments belong to enterprises

 ★ Assets formed through the Cooperative Development Fund（CDF）investments belong to cooperatives

 ★ There is a clear process for the disposal of non-performing assets，with property rights transferred to village collectives

Workshop and laboratory constructed with Project Grants（Guangxi Donglan Guilong Ecological Agriculture Technology Co.，Ltd）

Production Equipment Purchased with Project Grants（Guangxi Dahua Farui Village Yueteng Farmers' Professional Cooperative）

Cold Chain Transport Vehicles Purchased with Project Grants（Guangxi Bama Babaili Agriculture Co.，Ltd.）

Production Equipment Purchased with Project Grants（Baise Yimu Granary Agricultural Development Farmers' Professional Cooperative）

Overall Project Impact

I. The Project has been successfully selected as global poverty reduction cases

Project funds have been invested in mulberry planting and silkworm breeding farmers' professional cooperatives and edible fungus farmers' professional cooperatives with crushed mulberry stems as the base material in Yizhou District, Hechi City. These funds have boosted the sustainable and stable income growth of 18, 000 silkworm households. This case was selected as one of the best practices in the Fourth Call of Global Solicitation on Best Poverty Reduction Practices.

Full-process Support from Project Funds for the Sericulture Industry Value Chain

Mulberry planting

Young silkworm breeding

Cocooning

Silkworm cocoon collection

Silk reeling

Silk product sales

II. The promotional coverage and influence of the Project have increased

The promotional articles on the World Bank-Financed Project have been published by media outlets, including the *Economic Daily*, *Science and Technology Daily*, *Farmers' Daily*, *China County Times*, GXTV News channel, the New Economic Observation program, China Economic Net (www.ce.cn), and People's Daily Online (people.cn). The Project's achievement promotion coverage and influence have been significantly improved.

Mr. Josef Ernstberger, a Project Consultant of the World Bank and Senior Agricultural Economist, was awarded the 2020 Guangxi "Golden Silkball Friendship Award" by the People's Government of Guangxi Zhuang Autonomous Region for his important role in Guangxi's economic construction and social development in such work as the World Bank-Financed Project.

Mr. Josef Ernstberger, a Project Consultant of the World Bank and Senior Agricultural Economist, was awarded the 2020 Guangxi "Golden Silkball Friendship Award" by the People's Government of Guangxi Zhuang Autonomous Region. The picture shows Li Qingfa, a second-level inspector of the Foreign Capital Project Development Center, Rural Revitalization Administration of Guangxi Zhuang Autonomous Region, issuing the certificate of honor to Mr. Josef Ernstberger

Ⅲ. The practical experience of the Project has been popularized and applied

The Project's achievements, practices, and prospective improvement measures about the establishment of interest bonding mechanisms between enterprises and cooperatives and rural households, as well as the mechanism of uniting farmers and helping them develop, have been featured in Issue 116 of *Guangxi CPPCC Information* and received instructions from the autonomous region's leaders. The innovative practices and management models of the Project have not only been copied and applied to Guangxi's poverty alleviation and rural revitalization efforts but have also been promoted and applied in China's first foreign aid poverty alleviation project—the East Asia Poverty Reduction Cooperation Pilot Project. This has made a due contribution to telling China's poverty reduction stories and sharing China's experience in poverty reduction.

Villagers of Xienglorm Village, Luang Prabang District, Laos, in the East Asia Poverty Reduction Cooperation Pilot Project, are using participatory methods to design industrial development projects within the village

Drawing on the public notice system of the World Bank-Financed Project, the East Asia Poverty Reduction Cooperation Pilot Project has set up bulletin boards on the exterior walls of the Activity Center of Xienglorm Village, Luang Prabang District, Laos, to publicly display the content of the project construction and the use of funds

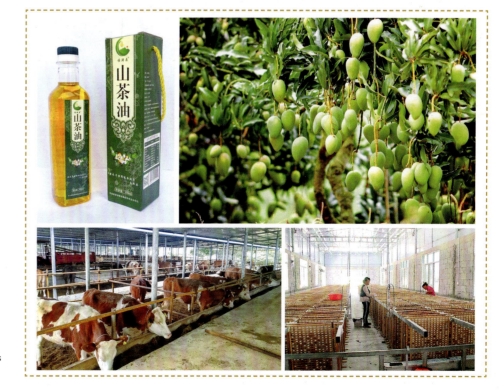

The Project supports industrial development and helps Guangxi in poverty alleviation and rural revitalization

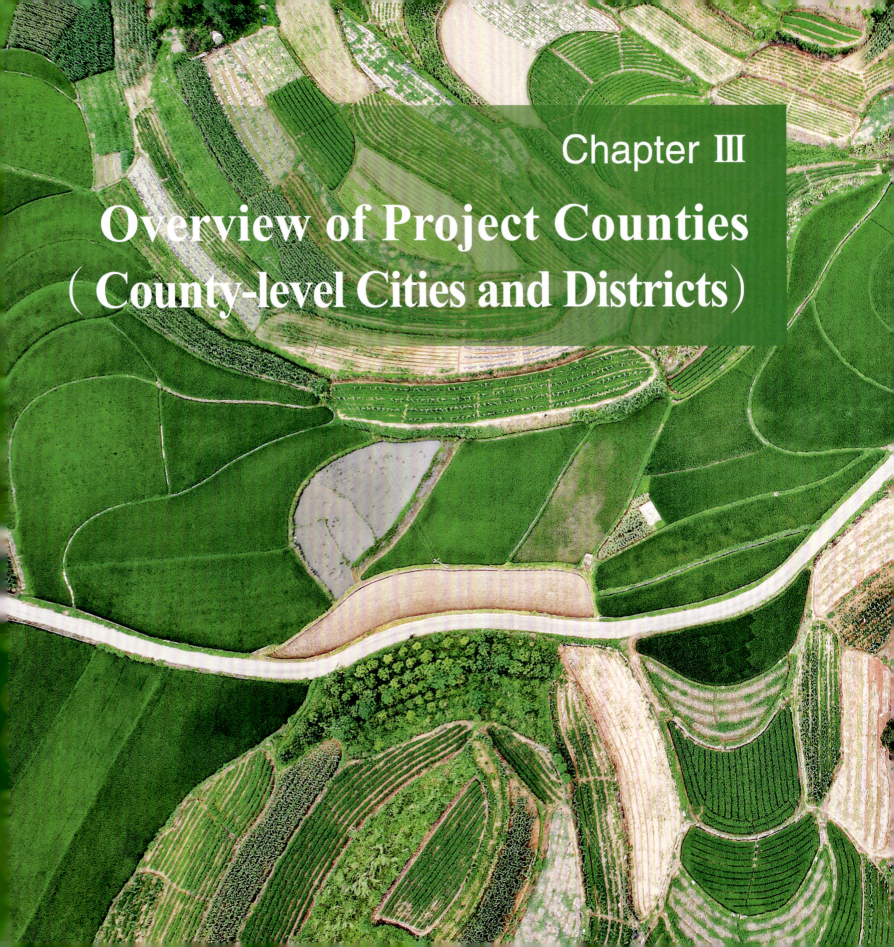

Chapter III
Overview of Project Counties
(County-level Cities and Districts)

Overview of the World Bank-Financed Project in Tiandong County

Project Overview

Located in the southwest of Guangxi, Tiandong County of Baise City was once a national key county for poverty alleviation and development. In 2017, Tiandong County launched the World Bank-Financed Project.

It successfully shook off poverty in 2019.

The World Bank-Financed Project in Tiandong County covers 14 administrative villages of 7 townships and towns, including 13 poverty-stricken villages (currently the villages have been lifted out of poverty). The project villages include Lianhe Village of Xiangzhou Town; Minzu Village of Linfeng Town; Liangyu Village, Dingyang Village, and Xinxu Village of Silin Town; Naban Village, Liaokun Village, and Lixin Village of Yincha Town; Xin'an Village, Daban Village, and Longxiang Village of Zuodeng Yao Township; Fuxing Village and Liuzhou Village of Naba Town; and Nahe Village of Yixu Town.

Areas covered by the Project

7 townships and towns and **14** administrative villages, including **13** poverty-stricken villages (currently the villages have been lifted out of poverty)

Population covered by the Project

Total population: **37,994**

Among them, **18,659** people were registered as poor (in 2017), **33,055** are ethnic minorities, and **20,244** are women

Investment for the World Bank-Financed Project in Tiandong County

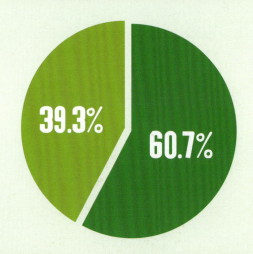

39.3%

60.7%

¥ **Domestic matching funds**
RMB **44.200** million yuan

¥ **Loans from the World Bank**
RMB **68.274** million yuan

Project Achievements

By the end of 2023

The company had signed linkage agreements
with **26** cooperatives in Tiandong
County, including **8** project cooperatives

The number of households benefited
5,899

The number of households lifted out of poverty
1,423

The number of households exceeding the monitoring target value
753

Mango purchased by company
10,400 tons

Output of mango juice
5,800 tons

I. A tripartite interest linkage mechanism has been established, with remarkable results achieved in enterprises' efforts to drive and benefit farmers

Guangxi Xianyou Agricultural Development Co., Ltd. is an enterprise implementing the Matching Grant Sub-project of the World Bank-Financed Project in Tiandong County. By adopting the "company + cooperatives + rural households/households lifted out of poverty" linkage mechanism, which benefits farmers and drives their development, the company has established a comprehensive partnership with cooperatives and rural households in planting, harvesting, storage, transportation, processing, and other links. It purchases inferior mango fruits from the cooperatives and their members under a "Minimum Price Guarantee, Market Price Procurement" agreement. These mangoes, which account for 20%-30% of the total, are slightly inferior in appearance and size compared with commercial mangoes but face fewer sales channels. This initiative has expanded the fruit marketing channels for local fruit farmers, increased rural households' income, consolidated the achievements of poverty alleviation, and at the same time, improved and extended the fruit industry chain, increased the added value of fruit products, and promoted the sustainable development of the fruit industry in Tiandong County. The effort has achieved comprehensive effects such as revitalizing the development of rural industries, increasing rural households' income, enhancing enterprise efficiency, and increasing the government's fiscal revenue.

Mango Processing Workshop

Mango Processing Enterprises Driving Rural Households to Increase Their Income

Work Site of the Mango Deep Processing Base of Guangxi Xianyou Agricultural Development Co., Ltd.

II. The Project has promoted the sustainable development of cooperatives and effectively enhanced the added value of industries

1. Infrastructure construction has been carried out

By the end of 2023, the following infrastructure had been constructed in 14 project villages

46, totaling **52.694** km  Access and Production roads

119, totaling **4,297.6** m³ Water tanks

Duck Shed at the Cooperative During Construction (Above) and After Construction (Below)

2. Expert advisory services have been provided

A database of experts and a database of potential service recipients have been established at the Tiandong County Business Service Center to offer professional and technical support in fields such as mango planting, mulberry planting, silkworm breeding, marketing, legal affairs, etc., to promote the development of cooperatives.

☆ **116** targeted services have been provided to cooperatives

☆ **12** advisory services have been offered to the public

On-site Training and Guidance by Financial Experts from Tiandong County Business Incubation Center at Liangyu Village

Tiandong County Organizing Mango Experts to Provide Technical Guidance to Growers

45

3. Efforts have been made to certify agricultural products and strengthen the management of industrial chain risks

Support has been provided to 6 cooperatives to obtain green food certification, and cooperatives have been supported to conduct agricultural product packaging design, register trademarks, purchase commercial insurance, etc., to boost the market competitiveness and risk prevention capabilities of the cooperatives' products. In addition, credit ratings for 4, 009 rural households and asset appraisals for 14 cooperatives have been completed.

☆ Credit ratings completed for **4,009** households

☆ Asset appraisals carried out for **14** cooperatives

Tiandong County Strengthening Industrial Chain Risk Management (Food and Drug Testing Institute)

Guangxi Tiandong Chuangfu Mulberry Planting and Silkworm Breeding Professional Cooperative Continuously Improving Product Risk Prevention Ability

Guangxi Tiandong Zihe Planting and Breeding Farmers' Professional Cooperative

4. Efforts have been made to strengthen capacity building and expand sales channels

Training in planting and breeding techniques, business operation and management, and e-commerce livestreaming has been organized through the Business Service Center, with a total of 979 participants trained, enhancing the operation and management capabilities of rural households, cooperatives, and local enterprises. Participation in agricultural trade fairs has been organized, along with 28 visits for cooperatives and enterprises to go both inside and outside of Guangxi for investigation, study, exchange, and cooperation, promoting cooperatives and enterprises to reach cooperation with other enterprises and individuals.

Participation in regional and other related trade fairs

 Promoting

Income from mangoes: RMB **371, 100** yuan

Income from camellia oil: RMB **32, 000** yuan

Income from silkworm cocoons: RMB **115, 900** yuan

Tiandong County Organizing a Project Investigation Outside the County

5. Many honorary titles have been received

With the support of the World Bank-Financed Project, Tiandong Jufuyuan Modern Agriculture Planting and Breeding Farmers' Professional Cooperative was awarded as a demonstration cooperative for farmers in Baise City in 2019, a regional demonstration cooperative in 2020, and a national demonstration cooperative in 2022. Chuangfu Mulberry Planting and Silkworm Breeding Professional Cooperative and Xiangzhou Lianqiang Planting and Breeding Farmers' Professional Cooperative in Tiandong County, Guangxi were honored as demonstration cooperatives for farmers in Baise City in 2021.

Honors Received by Guangxi Tiandong Chuangfu Mulberry Planting and Silkworm Breeding Professional Cooperative

Overview of the World Bank-Financed Project in Pingguo City

Project Overview

Located in the southwest of Guangxi, Pingguo City of Baise City was designated in 2012 as a planned county in the rocky desertification area of Yunnan, Guangxi, and Guizhou. In 2017, Pingguo County（it was officially upgraded to a county-level city on 26th, December 2019）launched the World Bank-Financed Project.

The World Bank-Financed Project in Pingguo City covers 11 administrative villages of 8 townships and towns, namely Ponan Village of Xin'an Town; Balong Village and Burong Village of Guohua Town; Linlin Village and Chami Village of Taiping Town; Yongqi Village of Haicheng Township; Longban Village of Pozao Town; Xingeng Village and Liu'an Village of Jiucheng Town; Longpai Village of Fengwu Town; and Yongwang Village of Bangxu Town.

 **Areas covered by the Project**

8 townships and towns and **11** administrative villages that were all poverty-stricken villages（currently the villages have been lifted out of poverty）

Population covered by the Project

Total population：**21,220**

Among them，**6,294** people were registered as poor（in 2017），**21,032** are ethnic minorities，and **7,317** are women

Investment for the World Bank-Financed Project in Pingguo City

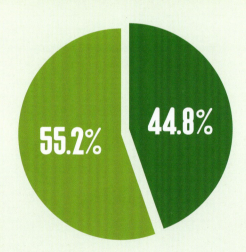

55.2%　44.8%

¥ **Domestic matching funds**
RMB **44.200** million yuan

¥ **Loans from the World Bank**
RMB **35.924** million yuan

Project Achievements

28 production access roads had been built totaling **32.18** kilometers

95 utility poles had been installed

13,309.7 meters of electrical wires had been laid

35,851 people from were benefited

9 drainage ditches had been built totaling **6,604.48** meters

14 water tanks（water towers）had been constructed totaling **2,194.47** cubic meters

I. Efficient progress has been made in constructing rural public infrastructure, thereby improving production conditions for cooperatives

By the end of 2023，28 production access roads with a total length of 32.18 kilometers had been built in 16 project villages；95 utility poles had been installed and 13,309.7 meters of electrical wires had been laid. Additionally，9 drainage ditches totaling 6,604.48 meters had been built，and 14 water tanks（water towers）with a total capacity of 2,194.47 cubic meters had been constructed. All these efforts have benefited 35,851 people.

Guangxi Pingguo Ruiyan Breeding Farmers' Professional Cooperative Before the Construction Power Facilities（Left）and After the Construction Power Facilities（Right）

Longchou Industrial Road Supported by the World Bank-Financed Project in Jilin Village，Taiping Town，Pingguo City Before the Construction of Production Roads（Left）and After the Construction of Production Roads（Right）

II. A mechanism has been built to link the interests of cooperatives and rural households，thus promoting the development of local characteristic industries

1. The land income of farmers has increased

Cooperatives in the Project implementation area

The number of households involved **537**

The area of land leased **810.95** mu*

The amount of land rental income received RMB **763,800** yuan

Pingguo Lvran Ecological Agriculture Professional Cooperative Paying Land Rent to Rural Households

Pingguo Fengying Ecological Agriculture Professional Cooperative Paying Land Rent to Rural Households

2. The income from labor collaboration has increased

Priority has been given to hiring cooperative members to work in the cooperatives，driving the development of 225 member households in total，and bringing an income of RMB 1.8543 million yuan.

Members of Pingguo Fengying Ecological Agriculture Professional Cooperative Earning Income by Fertilizing and Managing Mulberry

Guangxi Pingguo Nongdong Planting and Breeding Professional Cooperative Increasing Its Members' Income by Harvesting Forage Grass

---

* "Mu" is not a legal unit of measurement. 1 mu is approximately equal to 666.67 square meters.

3. Door-to-door purchase of agricultural products has been carried out to achieve win-win results

Cooperatives have directly purchased agricultural products such as corn and soybeans from their members and rural households for livestock and poultry breeding. They have purchased a total of 22.25 tons of agricultural products and paid a total of RMB 66,800 yuan, which has increased the income of their members and rural households.

🌾 Agricultural products purchased

22.25 tons

¥ Payment RMB

66,800 yuan

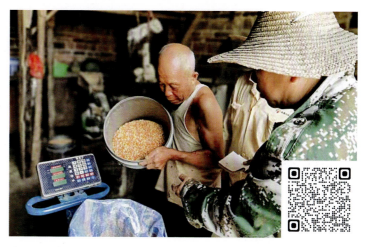

Pingguo Fuhengfei Pigeon Breeding Farmers' Professional Cooperative Purchasing Corn from Rural Households

4. Services have been provided to lower costs

Cooperatives have provided their members with services for the purchase of agricultural means of production and the sale and processing of agricultural products, aiming to save transaction costs and reduce production expenses.

By the end of 2023, the project cooperatives in Pingguo City had a total of 1,433 members, including 834 from households lifted out of poverty. The cooperatives raise 740 beef cattle, 115 breeding cattle, and 34 newborn calves; maintain 356 breeding sheep and 300 newborn lambs; raise 5,300 pairs of breeding pigeons, 2,200 pairs of young pigeons, and 11,635 squabs; and manage 1,250 mu of forage grass and 134 mu of mulberry fields. The annual output value of the 9 cooperatives supported by the project funds reached RMB 6,714,800 yuan.

Cattle Farm of Guangxi Pingguo Nongdong Planting and Breeding Professional Cooperative

Discussion Meeting on Calf Procurement at Pingguo Yongmin Planting and Breeding Farmers' Professional Cooperative

III. Targeted capacity building has been carried out to enhance the sustainable development capabilities of project participants

1. Sustainable development capabilities have been enhanced

A total of 161 participants in 8 batches—including staff from the PMO and Business Incubation Center, and cooperative counselors and managers—were organized to visit counties and cities of Guangxi such as Nanning, Hechi, Chongzuo, Pingxiang, and Leye, as well as provinces such as Guizhou and Yunnan, for investigation and study. A total of 14 sessions of training were conducted for cooperatives' procurement, finance, operation and management, and livestock and poultry breeding techniques, with 782 participants, further enhancing the cooperatives' self-organization, self-management, and self-supervision capacities for sustainable development.

2. The operation and management capabilities have been enhanced

The Business Incubation Center established under the support of the Project provides services for the development and startup of small and micro-sized enterprises and cooperatives in Pingguo City. By the end of 2023, a total of 432 participants had been trained in industrial skills, financial management, and business operation and management; the center had provided 97 services in total, enhancing the operation and management capabilities of rural households, cooperatives, and local small and micro-sized enterprises.

PMO of Pingguo County Visiting Chongzuo City and Pingxiang City for Investigation, Study, and Exchange

Industrial Skills Training for Cooperatives of Pingguo World Bank Loan Project Business Incubation Co., Ltd.

IV. Industrial chain risk management has been strengthened to improve the market competitiveness of agricultural products and their ability to prevent risks

By the end of 2023, with the support of project funds, 7 products and 14 trademarks had been designed and registered. Livestock and poultry disease prevention and control service organizations were hired for 7 breeding cooperatives, and commercial insurances were purchased for 1,913 heads of cattle and sheep.

Livestock and Poultry Disease Prevention and Control Experts Visiting Pingguo Baling Agriculture Professional Cooperative to Provide Guidance on Epidemic Disease Detection and Breeding Techniques

Trademark Registration

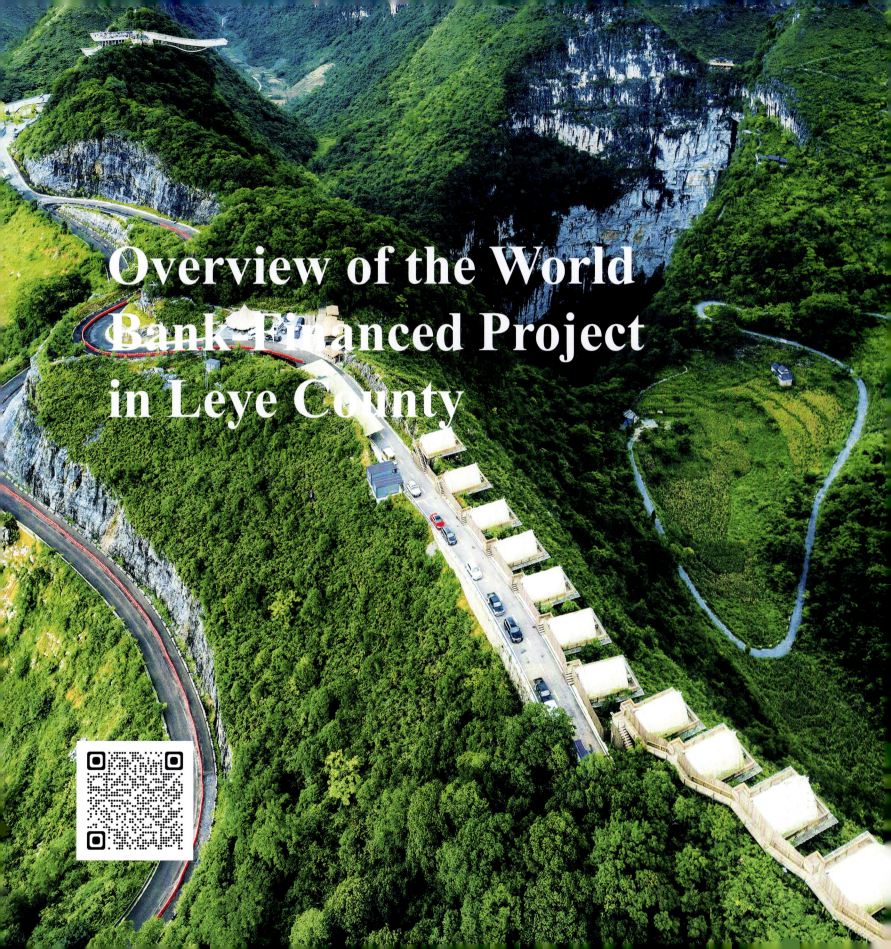

Overview of the World Bank Financed Project in Leye County

Project Overview

Located in the northwest of Guangxi, Leye County of Baise City is situated in the rocky desertification area of Yunnan, Guangxi, and Guizhou. Leye County, affected by the construction of the Longtan Reservoir, is a former revolutionary base of the CPC, and a demonstration base for organic agriculture. It was once a national key county for poverty alleviation and development and a county suffering from serious poverty. In 2017, Leye County launched the World Bank-Financed Project.

It successfully shook off poverty in 2020.

The World Bank-Financed Project in Leye County covers 12 administrative villages of 6 townships and towns, all of which were poverty-stricken villages (currently all these villages have been lifted out of poverty). The project villages include Dacun Village and Shuaba Village of Tongle Town; Dadao Village and Banhong Village of Gantian Town; Tangying Village and Quanda Village of Luosha Township; Linli Village and Nashe Village of Xinhua Town; Huayan Village and Yunlai Village of Huaping Town; and Qigeng Village and Minzhi Village of Luoxi Township.

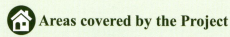

Areas covered by the Project

6 townships and towns and **12** administrative villages that were all poverty-stricken villages (currently the villages have been lifted out of poverty)

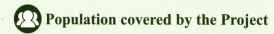

Population covered by the Project

Total population: **24,186**

Among them, **11,827** people were registered as poor (in 2017), **10,641** are ethnic minorities, and **10,598** are women

Investment for the World Bank-Financed Project in Leye County

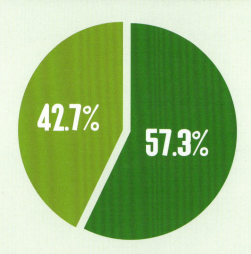

42.7%

57.3%

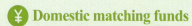

¥ Domestic matching funds

RMB **44.200** million yuan

¥ Loans from the World Bank

RMB **59.301** million yuan

Project Achievements

By the end of 2023, a total of 12 cooperatives with 1,870 members had been supported, including 1,250 members from households lifted out of poverty and 829 women. The Leye Sensen Ecological Beef Cattle Breeding Professional Cooperative and 3 leading agricultural enterprises, namely, Guangxi Leye Huadong Investment Co., Ltd., Leye County Caowangshan Tea Industry Co., Ltd., and Leye County Hengyuan Ecological Agriculture Comprehensive Development Co., Ltd. supported by the Project won the title of "Guangxi Modern Characteristic Agriculture Demonstration Zone". Leye County Jiajiaxiang Camellia Oil Farmers' Professional Cooperative was rated as a demonstration cooperative of Guangxi Farmers' Professional Cooperatives.

I. Efforts have been made to give full play to the radiating and driving role of project funds to promote enterprises and cooperatives in uniting farmers and helping them develop

With the support of the Project, 12 cooperatives and 3 enterprises have planted 1,374 mu of kiwifruit, 10,833 mu of camellia oleifera, and 956.20 mu of tea, raised 1,150 beef cattle, processed 8,000 tons of water-soluble fertilizer every year, and deeply processed 500 tons of organic tea every year.

12 cooperatives **+3** enterprises

Total Investment: RMB

103.501 million yuan

The number of cooperative members | The number of members from households lifted out of poverty

1,870 ➡ **1,250**

Leye Jiajiaxiang Camellia Oil Farmers' Professional Cooperative was rated as a demonstration cooperative of Guangxi Farmers' Professional Cooperatives

Leye Jiajiaxiang Camellia Oil Farmers' Professional Cooperative has been recognized as a key recommended brand for high-quality agricultural products.

II. Efforts have been made to select industrial projects to be supported and vigorously develop green and circular agriculture

1. Green industries have been developed

The Project has supported the construction of a water-soluble fertilizer production and processing plant in the central area of the main kiwifruit industry park in Leye County, seamlessly integrating with the Leye County Beef Cattle Breeding Base (including a cattle breeding professional cooperative supported by the World Bank-Financed Project) and the solid organic fertilizer factory. Wastewater from the solid organic fertilizer factory, manure from local livestock breeding, and sugar-cane mud from sugar factories are used as raw materials. Through refined processing techniques such as crushing, mixing, reacting, and packaging, waste is converted into fertilizer. This process produces organic water-soluble fertilizer that meets national standards, which is used by the county's poverty alleviation industry parks and professional cooperatives—such as those for kiwifruit and tea—as well as by individual planting households to improve soil properties, enhance product quality, and build green, organic, and circular industries in Leye County.

Organic Water-soluble Fertilizer Produced by Guangxi Leye Hengyuan Ecological Agricultural Integrated Development Co., Ltd.

2. Professional certifications have been obtained

By the end of 2023, among the 12 project cooperatives:

10 obtained green food certificates

5 certified by Conversion to Organiz Food

2 obtained geographical indication certifications

All **12** cooperatives obtained trademark registration certificates

7 processing cooperatives obtained food production licenses

Kiwifruit Products of Leye Xinyu Planting Professional Cooperative Obtaining the Geographical Indication Certification of the People's Republic of China

III. Efforts have been made to improve infrastructure and supporting facilities and enhance the quality of public services

1. Infrastructure has been improved

By the end of 2023, the benefited industries included 5,321 mu of kiwifruit, 7,488 mu of camellia oleifera, 2,521 mu of star anise, 1,732 mu of tea, and 2,040 heads（pieces）of livestock.

Industrial Road of Quanda Village in Luosha Township, Leye County

The coverage of village-level public infrastructure projects supported by the Project by the end of 2023

12 projects in **6** towns   **36** roads

17 water storage tanks   **1** floodway

The number of households benefited

3,272, totaling
14,697 people

The number of households lifted out of poverty

2,027, totaling
9,547 people

2. Additional public services and supporting facilities have been provided

The Project has supported the establishment of the Leye County Business Incubation Center to provide services for the development and startup of existing enterprises. By the end of 2023, training on planting and breeding techniques and e-commerce livestreaming had been carried out for a total of 1,120 participants. Credit ratings for 4,000 rural households and asset appraisals for 12 cooperatives had been completed. With the support of the Project, three cooperatives obtained loans of RMB 3.48 million yuan, and 656 rural households who completed credit ratings borrowed a total of RMB 42.4678 million yuan from credit cooperatives.

The First Training on Practical Camellia Oleifera Planting Techniques in Qigeng Village, Luoxi Township, Leye County

IV. Efforts have been made to strengthen project internal management and cultivate local talent teams

Each cooperative has been equipped with a dedicated advisor to assist in the formulation and implementation of project investment plans. Professional financial personnel have been hired to strengthen the financial management of the cooperatives. The Leye County Project Management Office and key cooperative members have been organized to conduct three sessions of training and investigation on project implementation management，with a total of 74 participants，so as to enhance these participants' project management and self-development capabilities.

Opening Ceremony of the Study Tour to Leye County to Investigate the Role of the World Bank-Financed Project in Enhancing Cooperatives' Capacity Building

A Member of Leye Zhenxingyuan Planting and Breeding Professional Cooperative Beginning to Operate Equipment for Tea Processing After Receiving Training

Training Course on the Study Tour to Leye County to Investigate the Role of the World Bank-Financed Project in Enhancing Cooperatives' Capacity Building

Overview of the World Bank-Financed Project in Tianlin County

Project Overview

Located in the northwest of Guangxi, Tianlin County of Baise City is a national key assisted county for rural revitalization and a county in the rocky desertification area of Yunnan, Guangxi, and Guizhou. Most of its areas are mountainous and it was once a national key county for poverty alleviation and development. In 2017, Tianlin County launched the World Bank-Financed Project.

It successfully shook off poverty in 2019.

The World Bank-Financed Project in Tianlin County covers 18 administrative villages of 10 townships and towns, namely Bangan Village and Genbiao Village of Baile Township; Pingbu Village of Lizhou Yao Township; Wenhua Village of Leli Town; Bo'e Village and Zhetang Village of Badu Yao Township; Bazhong Village and Baheng Village of Zhemiao Township; Sanyao Village and Nongguang Village of Lucheng Yao Township; Laizhou Village, Shifu Village, and Nadu Village of Jiuzhou Town; Pingxi Village of Liulong Town; Xiao'ao Village of Langping Town; and Baxin Village, Balai Village, and Changjing Village of Ding'an Town.

 Areas covered by the Project

10 townships and towns and **18** administrative villages that were all poverty-stricken villages（currently the villages have been lifted out of poverty）

 Population covered by the Project

Total population：**27,563**

Among them，**12,745** people were registered as poor（in 2017），**20,944** are ethnic minorities, and **11,672** are women

Investment for the World Bank-Financed Project in Tianlin County

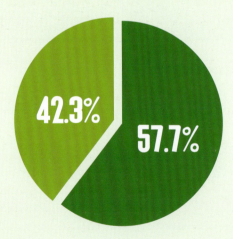

42.3%

57.7%

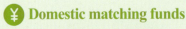

Domestic matching funds

RMB **44.200** million yuan

Loans from the World Bank

RMB **60.312** million yuan

Project Achievements

Camellia Oleifera of Tianlin Dakang Planting and Breeding Professional Cooperative

I. Efforts have been made to choose the types of industry to be developed based on local resources and planning

Tianlin County is rich in mountain resources and has the reputation of being "the hometown of camellia oleifera in China." The local people have a strong willingness to develop. Out of the 12 cooperatives supported by the Project, 10 are in the camellia oleifera industry. In addition, support has been given to Guangxi Tianlin County Xinfuyuan Camellia Oil Development Co., Ltd. to upgrade equipment and increase production capacity through the Matching Grant for Enterprises, which aligns with Tianlin's planning for the leading industry chain of camellia oleifera in the Implementation Plan for Consolidating and Expanding the Achievements of Poverty Alleviation and Effective Linkage with Rural Revitalization in National Key Assisted Counties for Rural Revitalization in Guangxi Zhuang Autonomous Region. The company has signed purchase agreements with 9 cooperatives (including 6 project cooperatives) and has cumulatively purchased 5,600 tons of camellia seeds from cooperatives and rural households, benefiting 2,239 rural households, including 550 households that have been lifted out of poverty.

The Project Supporting Guangxi Tianlin County Xinfuyuan Camellia Oil Development Co., Ltd. to Upgrade Equipment and Increase Production Capacity Through the Matching Grant for Enterprises

 Project cooperatives

 Xinfuyuan has signed contracts with

12 cooperatives

10 camellia oleifera cooperatives

9 cooperatives

6 project cooperatives

Camellia seeds purchased from cooperatives and rural households:

5,600 tons

The number of households benefited:

2,239

including **550** households have been lifted out of poverty

II. Industry chains have been extended and cross-regional brand cooperation has been conducted

Badu bamboo shoots are a famous specialty of Tianlin County and a national geographical indication product in China. The Project supports Tianlin Xingmao Badu Bamboo Shoots Planting Professional Cooperative in processing the bamboo shoots grown by rural households into sour bamboo shoots，which are supplied to relevant enterprises as an ingredient for Liuzhou luosifen（river snail rice noodles）. The annual supply amounts to 95, 281 kilograms，with a sales revenue of RMB 288, 300 yuan，benefiting 63 members and increasing their average annual income by RMB 4, 500 yuan.

Members of Tianlin Xingmao Badu Bamboo Shoots Planting Professional Cooperative Processing Bamboo Shoots

Members of Tianlin Xingmao Badu Bamboo Shoots Planting Professional Cooperative Drying Bamboo Shoots

Packaged Products of Badu Bamboo Shoots

Ⅲ. Infrastructure and public services have been improved，and risk management has been strengthened across the industry chain

1. Infrastructure construction has been carried out

The Project has supported the construction of 43 access roads and industrial roads totaling 133.05 kilometers and 40 water tanks in industrial areas，as well as drying fields for camellia seeds，comprehensive training buildings of cooperatives，etc. This has benefited 18 project villages and 3,393 rural households，including 1,185 households that have been lifted out of poverty.

The number of access roads and industrial roads

43
totaling
133.05 km

The number of water tanks in industrial areas
40

The number of households benefited
3,393

The number of households lifted out of poverty
1,185

Construction Project of the Gravel Road from Turnout of Shifu Village to Pearl Plum Industrial Base in Jiuzhou Town，Tianlin County

Hardening Project for the Road from Nanyan Valley to Meihua Mountain in Laizhou Village，Jiuzhou Town，Tianlin County

Hardening Project for Industrial Road from Baluntun Across Nalai Access Road to Citrus Base in Baxin Village，Ding'an Town，Tianlin County

2. Training efforts have been intensified

Efforts have been made to strengthen the capacity building of cooperatives. By the end of 2023, a total of 8 sessions of e-commerce training and industrial technology training had been organized，with a total of 659 trainees.

By the end of 2023

Organization of e-commerce training and industrial technology training
8 sessions

The number of trainees
659

2020 Training Course on Improving the Operation and Management Capabilities of Farmers' Professional Cooperatives Under the World Bank-Financed Project in Tianlin County

3. Product quality and market competitiveness have been enhanced

By the end of 2023, cooperatives had been supported to obtain 2 green food certificates and build 8 food safety monitoring rooms across the county to enhance local food safety monitoring capabilities: with the support of the Project, asset appraisal for 12 cooperative had been carried out, and Credit ratings for 4,583 rural households had been completed, help cooperatives and rural households improve their financing channels.

By the end of 2023

The number of green food certificates obtained by cooperatives
2

The number of food safety monitoring rooms built
8

Asset appraisal carried out for
12
cooperatives

Credit ratings completed for
4,583
households

Trademark Registration Certificates of Tianlin Pingbu Village Dakang Planting and Breeding Professional Cooperative

Agricultural Products Testing Room of Lizhou Yao Township in Tianlin County

Agricultural Products Testing Room of Bagui Institute of Market Supervision Administration of Tianlin County

4. Sales channels have been expanded

The Tianlin County Business Incubation Center has actively organized offline trade fairs, arranging for cooperatives and enterprises to hold or participate in 8 offline agricultural product exhibitions and sales events in Nanning and other cities. This initiative has facilitated cooperatives and enterprises to reach cooperation intentions with numerous merchants and individuals during the events, thereby expanding their sales channels.

5. E-commerce platforms have been developed

Efforts have been made to actively carry out e-commerce sales, set up livestreaming venues, and publicize the brands of cooperatives. Three livestreaming accounts were established on Douyin, Xigua Video, and Tencent, with nearly 30 livestreaming sessions conducted, contributing to the sale of 1,346 orders of agricultural products.

Product Raw Material Procurement of Guangxi Tianlin County Xinfuyuan Camellia Oil Development Co., Ltd.

Tianlin County Business Incubation Center and Partner Companies Conducting Live-streaming Marketing

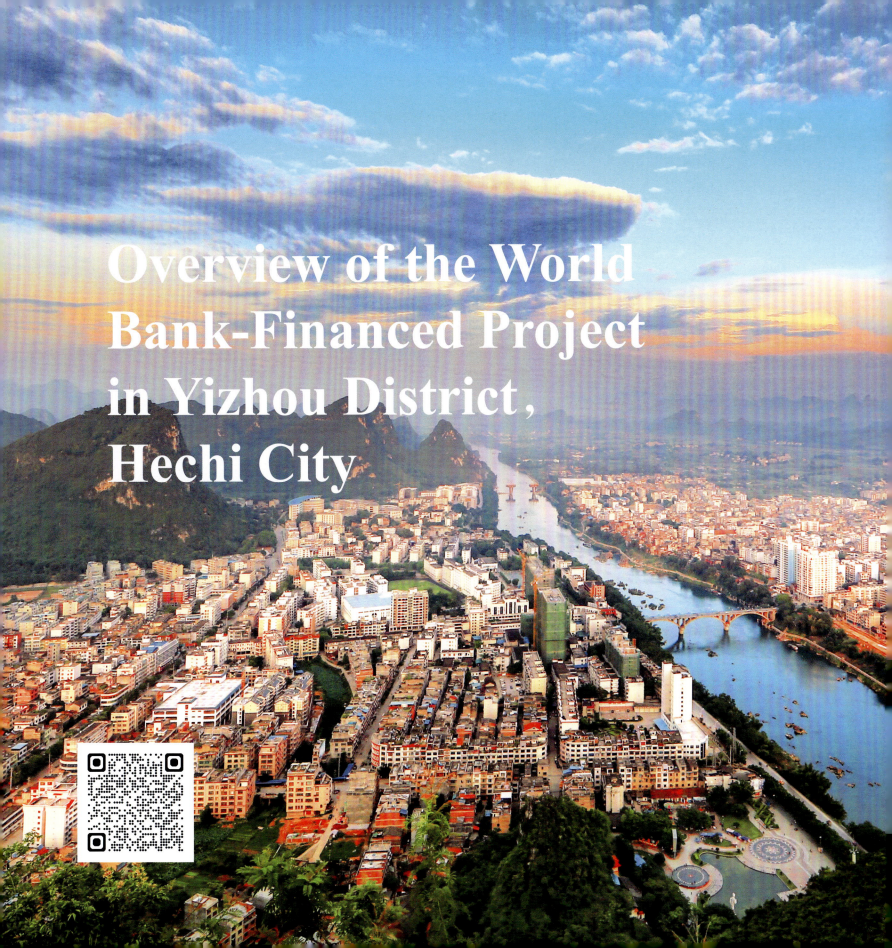

Overview of the World Bank-Financed Project in Yizhou District, Hechi City

Project Overview

Located in the north of central Guangxi, Yizhou District of Hechi City is the hometown of Liu Sanjie, a legendary folk singer of the Zhuang ethnic group. In 2017, Yizhou District launched the World Bank-Financed Project.

The World Bank-Financed Project in Yizhou District covers 14 administrative villages of 8 townships and towns, including 11 poverty-stricken villages (currently the villages have been lifted out of poverty). The project villages include Gudong Village of Liusanjie Town; Luofu Village of Luoxi Town; Lidong Village and Baiwei Village of Xiangbei Township; Gaoshou Village and Longtian Village of Longtou Township; Bailong Village, Baokang Village, Pandong Village, Douzhu Village and Shalang Village of Beiya Yao Township; Bochuan Village of Beishan Town; Longhou Village of Fulong Yao Township; and Yemao Village of Qingyuan Town.

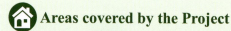

Areas covered by the Project

8 townships and towns and **14** administrative villages, including

11 poverty-stricken villages
(currently the villages have been lifted out of poverty)

Population covered by the Project

Total population: **39,110**

Among them, **9,903** people were registered as poor (in 2017),
32,868 are ethnic minorities, and **19,353** are women

Investment for the World Bank-Financed Project in Yizhou District, Hechi City

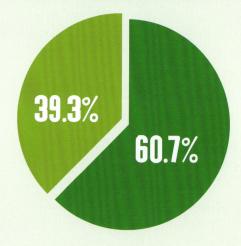

39.3%

60.7%

¥ **Domestic matching funds**

RMB **44.200** million yuan

¥ **Loans from the World Bank**

RMB **68.274** million yuan

Project Achievements

I. The business model of "cooperatives + bases + rural households" has been adopted to increase farmers' income

Cooperatives have been formed to help rural households expand production and business scales, improve the quality of agricultural products, and reduce production costs. By employing standardized production demonstration practices, providing planting and breeding technique training, and offering employment opportunities, the Project has helped increase income for those who have been lifted out of poverty. By the end of 2023, with the support of the Project, 14 cooperatives had been established, with 5 of them subsequently rated as reginal and city-level demonstration farmers' professional cooperatives; cooperation agreements had been signed with 38 cooperatives and village collectives, benefiting 35,789 farmers. The 14 cooperatives have added over 90 long-term jobs and more than 400 short-term jobs, effectively increasing the employment income of member rural households.

The number of cooperatives established	The number of demonstration professional farmers' cooperatives	The number of cooperatives and village collectives with cooperation agreements	The number of farmers benefited
14 →	**5**	**38** →	**35,789**

Hechi Yizhou Hanchangyi Breeding Professional Cooperative Creating More Jobs for Rural Households

Dividend Distribution at Hechi Yizhou Hanchangyi Breeding Professional Cooperative

II. Efforts have been made to improve the mechanism of uniting farmers and helping them develop by leading enterprises

Focusing on Yizhou District's pillar industries of mulberry planting, silkworm breeding, and silk production, the Project has supported Guangxi Jialian Silk Co., Ltd. and Guangxi Wehand-Bio Pharmaceutical Co., Ltd., two leading enterprises in agricultural industrialization, in implementing technical transformation and capacity expansion, enhancing their comprehensive strength, creating over 100 new construction jobs, adding over 50 new production positions to expand production capacity, and offering a significant number of temporary jobs.

The "leading enterprises + cooperatives + bases + rural households (including households lifted out of poverty)" cooperative development model has been adopted, concentrating on the development of contract farming, and vigorously promoting the application and demonstration of standardized mulberry planting and silkworm breeding techniques. This model utilizes industrial advancements to nurture the agricultural sector, strengthening the interest linkage with silkworm farmers, and fully leveraging the leading enterprises' role in increasing farmers' incomes. Cooperation agreements have been signed with 38 cooperatives, which have directly driven the construction of 30,000 mu of silkworm bases surrounding the enterprises. This has benefited 42,284 rural households, including 7,136 households that have been lifted out of poverty. In 2023, 5,064.0 tons of silkworm cocoons and 14,465.4 tons of mulberry trees were purchased from cooperatives and rural households, driving rural households to increase their income by RMB 300 yuan per mu of mulberry stems.

Guangxi Jialian Silk Co., Ltd. Receiving Project Grants to Expand Production Capacity and Increase Production Jobs

Enterprises Purchasing Silkworm Cocoons from Rural Households of Cooperatives to Increase Their Income

The number of cooperatives with cooperation agreements

38

Construction of silkworm bases surrounding the enterprises

30,000 mu

The number of households benefited

42,284

The number of households lifted out of poverty

7,136

In 2023

Silkworm cocoons purchased from cooperatives and rural households

5,064.0 tons

Increase in rural households' income per mu of mulberry stems

Mulberry trees

14,465.4 tons

RMB 300 yuan

Ⅲ. Infrastructure has been improved around industrial development

By the end of 2023，a total of 104 public infrastructure projects had been completed，including 23 hardened access road projects totaling 27.71 kilometers，19 industrial road projects totaling 27.10 kilometers，12 safety guardrail projects totaling 13.79 kilometers，3 water tank projects，19 water channel maintenance projects，15 drinking water safety guarantee projects，and 13 other projects，significantly improving the production and living conditions of project villages.

The number of project villages benefited
32

The number of households benefited:
7,906
totaling
27,193
people

The number of households lifted out of poverty
479
totaling
5,217
people

Chanye Road，Gaoshou Village，Longtou Township，Yizhou District，Hechi City

Ⅳ. Risk management has been strengthened across the industry chain

1. Food safety monitoring capabilities have been enhanced

By the end of 2023，two cooperatives had obtained organic product certification and two had passed green food certification. Food safety testing equipment had been purchased for food safety supervision and management units in Yizhou District to improve their food safety monitoring capabilities.

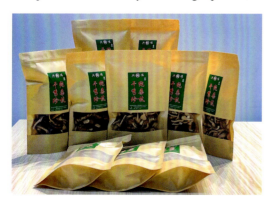

The certified "Green Food" products of Xingwei Planting and Breeding Professional Cooperative，Yizhou District，Hechi City

Organic Product Certificate

Green Food Certificate

2. Technical and management training has been strengthened

Yizhou District Business Incubation Center has provided targeted services for the development and startup of existing cooperatives and enterprises. By the end of 2023, practical training on mulberry planting and silkworm breeding techniques, business management training, and financial management training had been conducted for a total of 1,535 participants, enhancing the operation and management capabilities of rural households, cooperatives, and local enterprises. Cooperatives had been organized to participate in trade fairs held by various counties (districts) nine times.

Hechi Yuanyuan Planting and Breeding Professional Cooperative Holding a Training Session on the Digital System of the Agriculture-Commerce Alliance

3. Industrial development capital issues have been addressed

In combination with the "five-in-one" credit system construction carried out in Yizhou District, the project funds were used to actively conduct credit ratings for rural households and asset appraisals for cooperatives. The credit ratings for rural households have been completed with high quality in more than 20 administrative villages. As a result, 20,000 rural households received credit ratings from commercial financial institutions, and 86% of them were rated as high-quality, making them eligible for loans of up to RMB 50,000 yuan from financial institutions. This has effectively addressed the capital bottleneck problem for rural households developing their industries.

Aiming at the harmonious development of breeding efficiency with the ecological environment, research revolving around the beef cattle breeding industry has been conducted, putting forward scientific suggestions for enhancing the breeding efficiency of beef cattle. Relevant research outcomes have been utilized by beef cattle farmers in Yizhou District.

Breeding Technology Companies Putting Forward Scientific Suggestions on Beef Cattle Breeding to Cooperatives

Breeding Base of Hechi Yizhou Wanjiafu Breeding Professional Cooperative

Overview of the World Bank-Financed Project in Donglan County

Project Overview

Located in the northwest of Guangxi, Donglan County of Hechi City is situated in the rocky desertification area of Yunnan, Guangxi, and Guizhou. Characterized by many mountains and relatively little arable land, the county has its residents dispersed across its numerous valleys and ridges. It is a former revolutionary base of the CPC county, which was once designated as a national key county for poverty alleviation and development and was suffering from serious poverty. In 2017, Donglan County launched the World Bank-Financed Project.

It successfully shook off poverty in 2019.

The World Bank-Financed Project in Donglan County covers 16 administrative villages of 7 townships and towns, including 9 poverty-stricken villages (currently the villages have been lifted out of poverty). The project villages include Nala Village, Nahe Village, Renhe Village and Changdong Village of Sanshi Town; Jiangdong Village and Weirong Village of Donglan Town; Banlao Village, Tongle Village, Liutong Village and Lashe Village of Aidong Town; Kunwang Village of Wuzhuan Town; Bandeng Village of Changle Town; Banlie Village, Qieheng Village and Yingxi Village of Qiexue Township; and Baying Village of Bachou Township.

Areas covered by the Project

7 townships and towns and **16** administrative villages that were all poverty-stricken villages
(currently the villages have been lifted out of poverty)

Population covered by the Project

Total population: **31,022**

Among them, **8,873** people were registered as poor (in 2017), **27,952** are ethnic minorities, and **14,227** are women

Investment for the World Bank-Financed Project in Donglan County

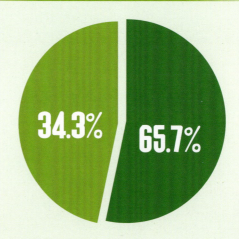

34.3%

65.7%

¥ **Domestic matching funds**

RMB **44.200** million yuan

¥ **Loans from the World Bank**

RMB **84.761** million yuan

Project Achievements

I. The development of characteristic industries has been boosted

1. Efforts have been made to support the development of farmers' professional cooperatives and enterprises

The Project has supported 16 farmers' professional cooperatives and 3 enterprises. It has restructured pillar agricultural industries to build demonstration planting and breeding industrial parks, upgraded existing planting and breeding industrial areas, and improved backward infrastructure, so as to promote the development of seven characteristic local industries, including the production of camellia oil, silkworms, medicinal materials, edible fungi, laying hens, broiler chickens, black goats, and beef cattle, and enhance the quality and efficiency these industries.

Camellia Oleifera Planting Base of Donglan Jiangdong Camellia Oleifera Farmers' Professional Cooperative

Oil Manufacture Equipment of Donglan Jiangdong Camellia Oleifera Farmers' Professional Cooperative

Camellia Oil Products of Donglan Jiangdong Camellia Oleifera Farmers' Professional Cooperative

Products at the Exhibition Hall of Guangxi Hefeng Pharmaceutical Co., Ltd.

Product of Guangxi Donglan Guilong Ecological Agriculture Technology Co., Ltd.—Shenxianshan Lotus Mushroom

Product of Guangxi Donglan Guilong Ecological Agriculture Technology Co., Ltd.—Agaric Sauce

Chickens Bred by Donglan Weirong Shunshun Ecological Agriculture Professional Cooperative

Goats Bred by Donglan County Baicaoyuan Ecological Goat Farming Cooperative

Cattle Bred by Donglan Leyi Planting and Breeding Professional Cooperative

2. Efforts have been made to support infrastructure construction

By the end of 2023

10 hardened roads
Totaling **11.939** km

8 gravel roads
Totaling **14.997** km

41 production access roads
Totaling **59.633** km

3 water channels
Totaling **2.237** km

25 water tanks
Totaling **3,610** m³

23 other facilities

Completion Acceptance of the Reservoir in Nala Village, Sanshi Town

II. A cooperation model featuring "enterprise leadership + cooperative operation + farmer participation" has been created

By the end of 2023, the 3 enterprises that received Matching Grants for Enterprises, including Guangxi Donglan Huashen Silk Co., Ltd., Guangxi Donglan Guilong Ecological Agriculture Technology Co., Ltd., and Guangxi Hefeng Pharmaceutical Co., Ltd., have signed cooperation agreements with 45 cooperatives and 177 village collectives, benefiting a total of 19,261 rural households.

Guangxi Donglan Huashen Silk Co., Ltd. Purchasing Silkworm Cocoons from Silkworm Farmers

Silk-making Workshop of Guangxi Donglan Huashen Silk Co., Ltd.

Farmers Going to the Fruiting Greenhouse of Guangxi Donglan Guilong Ecological Agriculture Technology Co., Ltd.

III. A mechanism of uniting farmers and helping them develop has been established to increase their income

There are 16 project cooperatives in Donglan County, of which 15 have realized dividend distribution, highlighting the remarkable effect of increasing farmers' income and effectively promoting rural revitalization.

2021 Dividend Conference of Baying Camellia Oleifera Planting Cooperative

Project cooperatives

The number of members
2,265

The number of lifted out of poverty
1,343

Cooperative dividends

1,985 people

1,217 people lifted out of poverty

Members benefited

Dividend amount RMB
1.2544 million

7,319
The highest dividend received

IV. Efforts have been made to improve the market competitiveness of cooperatives' products and their ability to prevent risks

By the end of 2023, the Project had supported cooperatives to obtain three camellia oleifera food production licenses, eight green food certificates, and 14 registered trademarks, helped seven cooperatives purchase commercial insurance, and purchased relevant equipment for food safety supervision and management units in Donglan County to improve local food safety monitoring capabilities.

Green Food Certificates Obtained by Cooperatives' Products

V. The quality of public services has been improved around industrial development

Donglan County Business Incubation Center has provided guidance and services for cooperatives, SME owners, returning entrepreneurs, and leaders of wealth-generating initiatives, with 200 instances of service provided. The Project supported Donglan County to cooperate with local financial institutions to establish a comprehensive credit rating system for rural households and cooperatives and carry out rural asset appraisals. By the end of 2023, 16 cooperatives had received asset appraisal services, and credit ratings had been completed for 4000 rural households.

Donglan County Business Incubation Center

★ Providing guidance and services for **200** persons

★ Asset appraisal carried out for **16** cooperatives

★ Credit ratings completed for **4,000** households

VI. Capacity building of Project Management Personnel has been strengthened

The Donglan County PMO has conducted 18 training sessions for 200 participants, including 120 project office managers and 80 cooperative managers. The training has further improved the capability of Donglan County's project managers in the brand-building of farmers' professional cooperatives, as well as rural development, rural construction, and rural governance through training courses such as those on agricultural industry development.

Training on Livestock and Poultry Disease Prevention and Control Held at the Foreign Capital Project Development Center of Donglan County on November 9, 2021

PMO of Donglan County Organizing and Holding the Technical Training of the Nahe Village Silkworm Breeding Professional Cooperative in Sanshi Town

PMO of Donglan County Organizing and Holding the First Capacity-building Training Course for Small and Medium-sized Enterprises, Farmers' Professional Cooperatives, and Entrepreneurship Pioneers

PMO of Donglan County Organizing Experts to Hold Training on Silkie Breeding Techniques in Niujiaopo Chestnut Under-forest Integrated Breeding Professional Cooperative in Aidong Town

Overview of the World Bank-Financed Project in Bama Yao Autonomous County

Project Overview

Located in the northwest of Guangxi, Bama Yao Autonomous County is situated in the rocky desertification area of Yunnan, Guangxi, and Guizhou. Aside from being the famed longevity village both domestically and worldwidely, Bama Yao Autonomous County is also a former revolutionary base area of the CPC and an area inhabited by ethnic minorities. Various factors have constrained its development. Moreover, it has a late start to development, a weak foundation, a large population, backward infrastructure, and seriously lagging industries. It was once a national key county for poverty alleviation and development. In 2017, Bama Yao Autonomous County launched the World Bank-Financed Project.

It successfully shook off poverty in 2020.

The World Bank-Financed Project in Bama Yao Autonomous County covers 14 administrative villages of 7 townships and towns, including 9 poverty-stricken villages (currently the villages have been lifted out of poverty). The project villages include Poteng Village, Shechang Village, Fafu Village, Panyang Village, and Jiemo Village of Bama Town; Yanting Village of Yandong Town; Donglie Village of Nashe Township; Pingliu Village of Suolue Township; Hele Village and Nongjing Village of Xishan Township; Changhe Village and Dena Village of Fenghuang Township; and Luopi Village and Pingtian Village of Bailin Township.

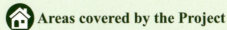

Areas covered by the Project

7 townships and towns and **14** administrative villages, including **9** poverty-stricken villages (currently the villages have been lifted out of poverty)

Population covered by the Project

Total population: **41,053**

Among them, **14,002** people were registered as poor (in 2017), **34,296** are ethnic minorities, and **17,714** are women

Investment for the World Bank-Financed Project in Bama Yao Autonomous County

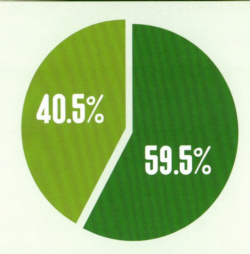

40.5%

59.5%

¥ **Domestic matching funds**
RMB **44.200** million yuan

¥ **Loans from the World Bank**
RMB **64.807** million yuan

Project Achievements

The Project supports

14 cooperatives

The Project benefits

2,166 households totaling **9,260** people

including **1,520** households totaling **6,615** people

lifted out of poverty, **1,960** ethnic minorities and

1,033 women

The Project develops

Goat breeding

Fragrant pig breeding

Broiler chicken breeding

Mulberry planting and silkworm breeding

Fruit planting

Camellia oleifera processing

Shouxiang cattle breeding

I. Remarkable achievements have been made in the construction of demonstration cooperatives

By the end of 2023, among the 14 cooperatives supported by the Project, 11 had achieved profitability. There had been 2 certifications for camellia oil cooperatives' food production licenses and 7 registered trademarks. Credit ratings for 2,166 rural households of the cooperatives had been completed. Since the implementation of the Project, 6 cooperatives have realized dividend distribution, totaling RMB 600,000 yuan, with 4 cooperatives having distributed dividends in the year 2023, amounting to RMB 300,000 yuan in total, benefiting 631 members (one person per household) and 404 households that have been lifted out of poverty.

Bama Zhongqing Planting and Breeding Farmers' Professional Cooperative and Guangxi Bama Jingfeng Planting and Breeding Farmers' Professional Cooperative were honored as region-level demonstration cooperatives in 2022. Guangxi Bama Fuxiu Planting and Breeding Farmers' Professional Cooperative was rated as the outstanding farmers' professional cooperative of Bama Yao Autonomous County and the demonstration cooperative of Hechi City in 2021.

During and After the Construction of Goat House of Guangxi Bama Nongwang Planting and Breeding Farmers' Professional Cooperative

Shouxiang Cattle of Bama Zhongqing Planting and Breeding Farmers' Professional Cooperative Growing Well

Chickens Perching Under the Forest at Guangxi Bama Jingfeng Planting and Breeding Farmers' Professional Cooperative

////// II. The Business Incubation Center has provided professional services //////

The Business Incubation Center of Bama Yao Autonomous County has provided specialized services such as training and teaching, registration and certification, business management and planning, legal consulting services, and financial services, as well as organized trade fairs and exchange meetings for the development of small and micro-sized enterprises and cooperatives. By the end of 2023, a total of 75 targeted services have been carried out, serving a total of 660 people.

Carrying out

75 targeted services for **660** people

Business Incubation Center of Bama Yao Autonomous County

Scene of the 2023 Nanning Trade Fair for Characteristic Agricultural Products of Bama Yao Autonomous County

2023 Training Course on E-commerce Livestreaming in Bama Yao Autonomous County

III. The matching grant for enterprises has played an obvious driving role

Guangxi Xiaogu Chicken Agriculture and Animal Husbandry Co., Ltd. and Guangxi Bama Babaili Agriculture Co., Ltd. in Bama Yao Autonomous County have been approved to receive project matching grants. The two companies have driven the development of 29 associated cooperatives, promoting the development of characteristic industries among 4,523 rural households. They have purchased 643,200 broiler chickens raised by cooperatives and rural households, and supplied 444,900 baby chicks. A total of 701 rural households have been motivated to participate in forage grass planting and straw recycling, including 121 households that have been lifted out of poverty.

Guangxi Xiaogu Chicken Agriculture and Animal Husbandry Co., Ltd.

Guangxi Bama Babaili Agriculture Co., Ltd.

Approved to receive project matching grants

Driving the development of
29 associated cooperatives

Purchasing
643,200 broiler chickens raised by cooperatives and rural households

Promoting the development of characteristic industries among
4,523 households

Supplying
444,900 baby chicks

Motivating
701 rural households to engage in forage grass planting and straw recycling

Helping
121 rural households lifted out of poverty

Industry Core Demonstration Area of Guangxi Xiaogu Chicken Agriculture and Animal Husbandry Co., Ltd.

Wagyu Breeding Base of Guangxi Bama Babaili Agriculture Co., Ltd.

Production Base of Guangxi Xiaogu Chicken Agriculture and Animal Husbandry Co., Ltd.

IV. The production and living conditions in the project area have been improved

By the end of 2023

Infrastructure construction

Production roads

57
123.6 km

Retaining walls

2,701.19 m³

Road hardening

56.27 m²

Guard railing

3.67 km

Production Road of Guangxi Bama Fuxiu Planting and Breeding Farmers' Professional Cooperative

Production Road of Camellia Oleifera Cooperative in Pingliu Village, Suolue Township, Bama Yao Autonomous County

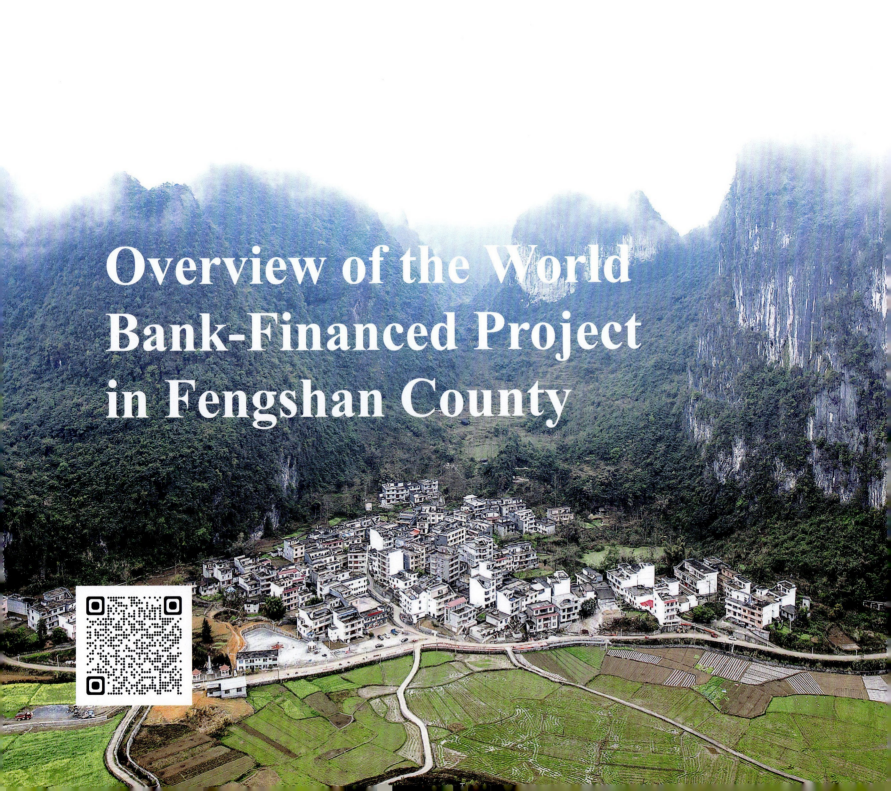

Overview of the World Bank-Financed Project in Fengshan County

Project Overview

Located in the northwest of Guangxi, Fengshan County of Hechi City is situated in the rocky desertification area of Yunnan, Guangxi, and Guizhou. It was once a national key county for poverty alleviation and development and a county suffering from serious poverty in Guangxi. In 2017, Fengshan County launched the World Bank-Financed Project.

It successfully shook off poverty in 2020.

The World Bank-Financed Project in Fengshan County covers 16 administrative villages of 4 townships and towns, including 14 poverty-stricken villages (currently the villages have been lifted out of poverty). The project villages include Nongzhe Village of Fengcheng Town; Gengsha Village, Pocha Village, and Longwang Village of Jinya Yao Ethnic Township; Nawang Village, Heyun Village, Shanglin Village, Tongle Village, and Wenli Village of Qiaoyin Township; and Banlun Village, Na'ai Village, Nalao Village, Nale Village, Changzhou Village, Langli Village, and Banren Village of Changzhou Town.

🏠 Areas covered by the Project

4 townships and towns and **16** administrative villages, including **14** poverty-stricken villages
(currently the villages have been lifted out of poverty)

👥 Population covered by the Project

Total population: **36,108**

Among them, **11,385** people were registered as poor (in 2017), **21,163** are ethnic minorities, and **15,833** are women

Investment for the World Bank-Financed Project in Fengshan County

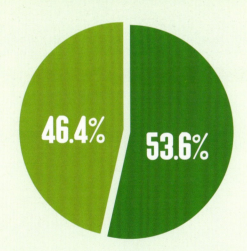

46.4% 53.6%

¥ **Domestic matching funds**

RMB **44.200** million yuan

¥ **Loans from the World Bank**

RMB **51.062** million yuan

Project Achievements

I. Positive results have been achieved in supporting the construction of cooperatives

By the end of 2023, the Project had supported the construction of 11 cooperatives, benefiting 780 people who have been lifted out of poverty, 924 ethnic minorities, and 718 women. Industries developed include camellia oleifera processing, chili sauce production, rice production and processing, walnut purchasing and processing, joint breeding of young silkworms, purchasing and drying of silkworm cocoons, five-color glutinous rice production, and pig breeding.

The number of cooperatives established under support

11

» The number of people lifted out of poverty
780

The number of ethnic minorities
924

The number of women
718

Production Equipment of Fengshan Chang'ai Camellia Oleifera Processing Professional Cooperative

Staff of Fengshan County Agricultural Products Rapid Testing Room Conducting Safety Inspections on Agricultural Products from Cooperatives

Pigs Bred by Fengshan Jiali Pig Breeding Professional Cooperative

Five-color Glutinous Rice Products of Fengshan Hongxing Walnut Farmer Professional Cooperative

Ⅱ. Matching grants have been provided to enterprises to strengthen the interest linkage and sharing with cooperatives and rural households

Matching grants have been provided to enterprises to strengthen the interest linkage and sharing with cooperatives and rural households through investment activities. By the end of 2023, cooperation agreements had been signed with nine cooperatives and village collectives, benefiting 2,252 rural households.

Honor Certificate Wall of Guangxi Fengshan Jiahong Seedling Co., Ltd.

Guangxi Fengshan Jiahong Seedling Co., Ltd. Purchasing Caulis Mahoniae from Rural Households

Demonstration Base for Caulis Mahoniae Planting in Fengshan County

Exhibits of Guangxi Fengshan Jiahong Seedling Co., Ltd.

Ⅲ. Infrastructure and public services have been improved

By the end of 2023，with the support of the Project，cooperatives had obtained 13 agricultural product certifications that include green food certificates and agro-product geographical indications，as well as completed packaging design and trademark registration for their products. Furthermore，six safety rapid testing labs for characteristic agricultural products in farmers' markets were constructed in the Jiangzhou，Pingle，Changzhou，Zhaiya，Jinya，and Siyuan communities. Relevant equipment had been purchased for food safety supervision and management units in Fengshan County to strengthen local food safety testing and monitoring.

The Project supports cooperation between Fengshan County and local financial institutions. By the end of 2023，credit ratings had been completed for 4,400 rural households，and 19 cooperatives had received asset appraisal services.

> **By the end of 2023，15 project villages had been supported to resolve the issue of difficult transportation of living and production water and agricultural products**

Production roads	Water channels	Reservoirs	Drying field for camellia seeds	Rubble masonry retaining walls
47	**15**	**217**	**1**	**168**
135.093 km	**18.482** km	**89,470** m³	**510** m²	**25,562** m³

Galvanized steel safety guardrails along village-level roads	Road repair	Hardening of cooperatives' sites	Drinking water pipeline	
12	**3**	**1,000** m²	**3,618** m	
9,060 m	**2,343** m²			

The Drinking Water Safety Consolidation and Improvement Project of Bayatun in Nawang Village，Qiaoyin Township，Completed on October 25，2021

Good Agricultural Practice Certification

Green Food Certificate of Camellia Oil

IV. Training has been strengthened to improve self-development abilities

By the end of 2023, the Fengshan County Business Incubation Center had conducted training on planting and breeding techniques, finance, capacity building, and we-media operation for a total of 1,162 participants, to enhance the operation and management capabilities of rural households, cooperatives, and local enterprises.

The Project has supported the county to organize study tours with a total of 118 participants to World Bank project cooperatives and industrial bases in regions such as Hunan, Guizhou and Fujian. These tours were aimed at learning the experience and practices of cooperative construction and sustainable operation from the advanced regions.

PMOs of Fengshan County Carrying out the Cooperative Technical Training Promotion Meeting

Fengshan County Rural Revitalization Bureau Visiting Hunan Province for Investigation, Study, and Exchange

V. Sales channels of agricultural products have been expanded

The Fengshan County Business Incubation Center has organized cooperatives and enterprises to hold or participate in offline agricultural product exhibitions and sales events in Guilin and Nanning. This initiative has facilitated cooperatives and enterprises to reach cooperation intentions with numerous enterprises and individuals during the events, thereby expanding their sales channels.

In November 2023, Fengshan County held the World Bank-Financed Project Characteristic Agricultural Products Exhibition and Sales Activity and the 2023 Guangxi Catering Culture Expo World Bank Special Promotion Conference with the theme of "Longevity Ingredients with Guangxi Flavors" in Guilin.

2023 Fengshan Characteristic Agricultural Product Trade Fair of the World Bank-Financed Project Held in Guilin

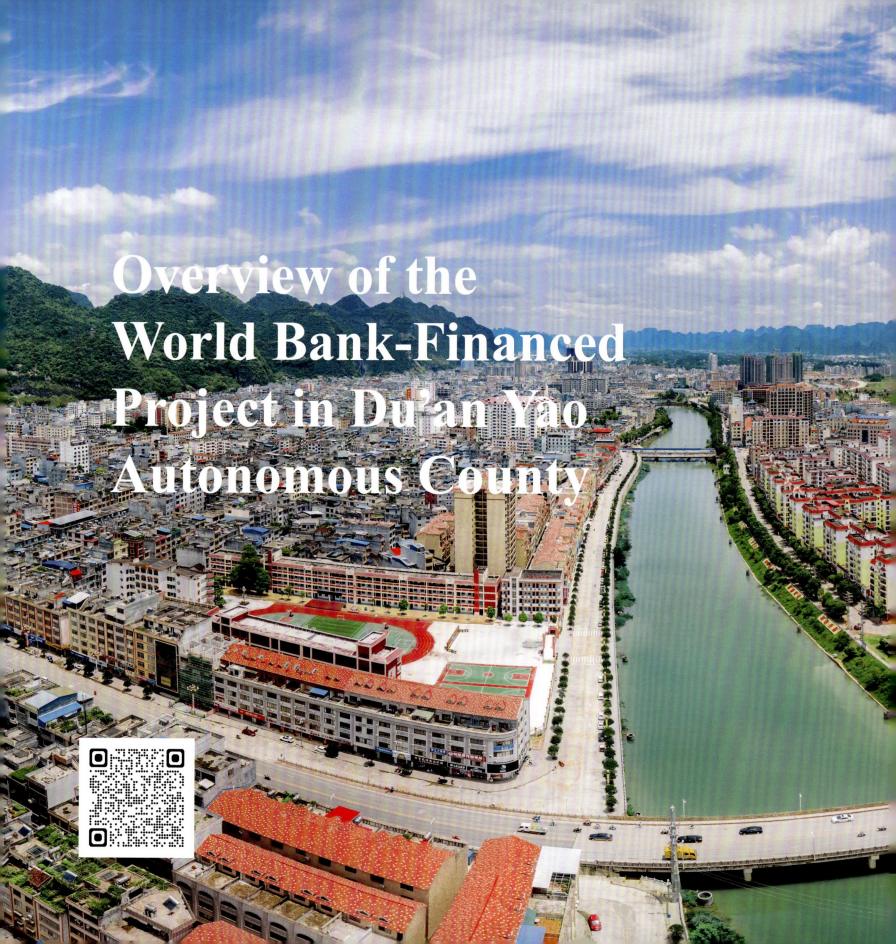

Overview of the
World Bank-Financed
Project in Du'an Yao
Autonomous County

Project Overview

Located in the west of central Guangxi, Du'an Yao Autonomous County lies in the rocky desertification area of Yunnan, Guangxi, and Guizhou. It was once a national key county for poverty alleviation and development, a national severe poverty-stricken county, and an extremely impoverished county in Guangxi. In 2017, Du'an Yao Autonomous County launched the World Bank-Financed Project.

It successfully shook off poverty in 2020.

The World Bank-Financed Project in Du'an Yao Autonomous County covers 15 administrative villages of 7 townships and towns, including 13 poverty-stricken villages (currently the villages have been lifted out of poverty). The project villages include Liuli Village and Ganwan Village of Chengjiang Town; Yuanli Village of Bao'an Township; Anle Village and Yongji Village of Yong'an Town; Wudong Village, Nongming Village, Fuxing Village, Jiating Village, Jiaquan Village, Yijiang Village, and Jiacha Village of Gaoling Town; Yingshan Village of Longwan Township; Longba Village of Xia'ao Town; and Anning Village of Dongmiao Township.

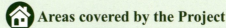

Areas covered by the Project

7 townships and towns and **15** administrative villages, including

13 poverty-stricken villages

(currently the villages have been lifted out of poverty)

Population covered by the Project

Total population: **34,447**

Among them, **9,950** people were registered as poor (in 2017), **26,072** are ethnic minorities, and **12,781** are women

Overview of the World Bank-Financed Project in Du'an Yao Autonomous County

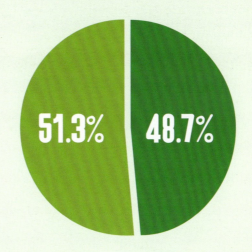

51.3%　48.7%

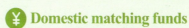

Domestic matching funds

RMB **44.200** million yuan

Loans from the World Bank

RMB **41.910** million yuan

91

Project Achievements

1. Cooperatives have established a linkage mechanism for the development of rural households

With the support of the Project, cooperatives have helped their members build chicken coops, goat houses, and silkworm houses and place orders for baby chicks in a unified manner. They have also provided members with free technical guidance on breeding, thus effectively helping them reduce production costs and risks.

The number of project-supported cooperatives

13

The number of cooperative members

1,485

The number of people from households lifted out of poverty

1,084

Industrial investment fields of the project-supported cooperatives

7 Du'an goat breeding cooperative, **1** mulberry planting and silkworm breeding cooperative, **2** pig breeding cooperatives, **1** beef cattle breeding cooperative, and **2** native free-range chicken

Guangxi Du'an Lvyin Mulberry Planting and Silkworm Breeding Professional Cooperative Distributing Mulberry Seedlings to Its Members

Chicken Raised by Du'an Bainong Free-Range Chicken Raising Professional Cooperative

Du'an Shengxing Ecological Breeding Professional Cooperative

Goat House of Du'an Xinglong Planting and Breeding Professional Cooperative

Interior of the Silkworm House of Du'an Lvyin Mulberry Planting and Silkworm Breeding Professional Cooperative

Yaoshan Cattle of Du'an Shengxing Ecological Breeding Professional Cooperative

//// II. Infrastructure and public services have been improved ///////////////

By the end of 2023，roads and water tanks had been built for 13 project villages to improve production and living conditions of local farmers. The Du'an Yao Autonomous County Business Incubation Center carried out 23 sessions of training on planting and breeding techniques，operation and management，and e-commerce livestreaming，with a total of 1, 077 participants. They have also provided cooperatives with professional technical consultation and technical training services 17 times，enhancing the operation and management capabilities and industry development confidence of rural households，cooperatives，and local enterprises.

Roads

63
54.903 km

Water tanks

44
11,600 m³

Training

23 sessions
1,077 participants

The Du'an Yao Autonomous County Business Incubation Center has hired full-time acting bookkeepers for project cooperatives to carry out unified financial account-keeping work，thereby strengthening the management of cooperatives' financial systems and effectively improving the standardization of cooperative management.

From April 28 to May 1，2023，the Du'an Yao Autonomous County Business Incubation Center held a trade fair for agricultural products of the World Bank-Financed Project in the Three Streets and Two Alleys of Nanning City. The event primarily promoted agricultural products and cultural tourism resources from various counties（cities，districts）involved in the Project. It helped the participating cooperatives and enterprises to reach cooperation intentions with numerous enterprises and individuals，thus expanding sales channels. On-site sales of agricultural and specialty products reached about RMB 200, 000 yuan，and strategic cooperation agreements amounting to RMB 25 million yuan were signed，of which the contract amount between Guangxi Aodu Agriculture and Animal Husbandry Technology Co.，Ltd. and Shenzhen Shouxiang Zhenpin Agricultural Development Co.，Ltd. reached RMB 10 million yuan.

"Lively Spring in Lovely Du'an"—2023 Direct Sales Activity of Agricultural and Specialty Products from Farmers' Professional Cooperatives and SMEs Supported by the World Bank-Financed Project

The First Training Course on Cattle and Goat Breeding Techniques（Guihequan Site）

Hardening Project for the Industrial Road from Jiaquan Village Xiapo to Nongji in Gaoling Town

The Second Training on E-commerce Operation for Farmers' Professional Cooperatives in 2021

III. Livestock and poultry disease prevention and control services have been offered to escort the development of cooperatives

The Du'an Yao Autonomous County PMO has hired third-party professional organizations to provide livestock and poultry disease prevention and control services for the project cooperatives, offering effective measures to deal with disease issues during the planting and breeding process, thereby reducing the planting and breeding risks faced by the cooperatives.

Livestock and Poultry Disease Prevention and Control and On-site Guidance by Guangxi Yuemu Biotechnology Co., Ltd.

IV. Financing channels have been improved

Efforts have been made to cooperate with local financial institutions to develop a comprehensive credit rating system for rural households and cooperatives, and third-party agencies have been hired to conduct asset appraisals for cooperatives. These ratings and appraisals help individual rural households and cooperatives meet the conditions for obtaining loans from designated financial institutions. By the end of 2023, credit ratings had been completed for 4053 rural households, and 11 cooperatives had received asset appraisal services.

Asset Appraisal Services

V. Capacity building has been strengthened

By the end of 2023，Du'an Yao Autonomous County had carried out

Training on planting and breeding techniques
Operation and management training
E-commerce live streaming training

23 sessions
1077 participants

Field investigation

7 sessions
78 participants

Visiting Guizhou Province for Investigation

Visiting the World Bank project in Gansu for Investigation

Visiting Bama Yao Autonomous County to Investigate the Operation of the Business Incubation Center

Visiting the World Bank-Financed Project in Dahua Yao Autonomous County for Investigation

Overview of the World Bank-Financed Project in Dahua Yao Autonomous County

Project Overview

Dahua Yao Autonomous County in Hechi City is located in the middle reaches of the Hongshui River in the northwest of central Guangxi. It lies in the rocky desertification area of Yunnan, Guangxi, and Guizhou. It was once a national key county for poverty alleviation and development and an extremely impoverished county in Guangxi. In 2017, Dahua Yao Autonomous County launched the World Bank-Financed Project.

It successfully shook off poverty in 2020.

The World Bank-Financed Project in Dahua Yao Autonomous County covers 11 administrative villages of 8 townships and towns, all of which were poverty-stricken villages (currently all these villages have been lifted out of poverty). The project villages include Datiao Village and Shuangpai Village of Dahua Town; Shangwu Village, Zhongwu Village, and Wucheng Village of Duyang Town; Jiasi Village of Liuye Township; Liushuo Village of Yantan Town; Jiankang Village of Qiangxu Township; Changhuai Village of Yixu Township; Nongxiong Village of Qibainong Township; and Farui Village of Jiangnan Township.

 Areas covered by the Project

8 townships and towns and **11** administrative villages that were all poverty-stricken villages (currently the villages have been lifted out of poverty)

 Population covered by the Project

Total population: **30,128**

Among them, **5,406** people were registered as poor (in 2017), **27,879** are ethnic minorities, and **13,219** are women

Investment for the World Bank-Financed Project in Dahua Yao Autonomous County

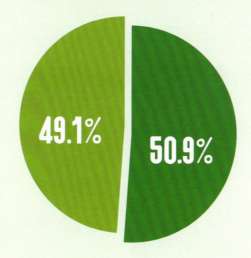

49.1%

50.9%

 Domestic matching funds

RMB **44.200** million yuan

 Loans from the World Bank

RMB **45.905** million yuan

97

Project Achievements

I. Infrastructure has been improved, highlighting the social benefits of the Project

By the end of 2023, 65 access and production roads totaling 85.412 kilometers, 51 water tanks with a total capacity of 8,850 cubic meters, and 4 sets of water conservancy irrigation channels had been built in 11 project villages to improve production and living conditions of local villagers.

Infrastructure construction in **11** project villages

Access and production roads	Water tanks	Water conservancy irrigation channels
65	**51**	**4**
85.412 km	**8,850** m³	

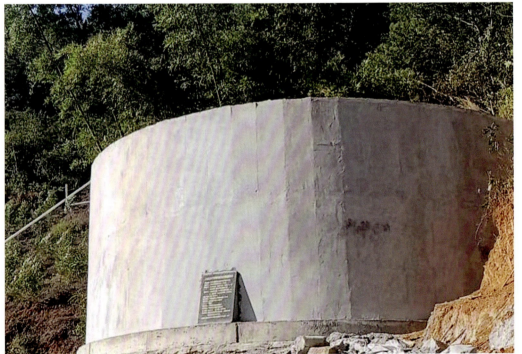

Human and Livestock Drinking Water Project of Kangzhida Cooperative in Jiankang Village, Qiangxu Township

Road Hardening in Paixiatun of Shuangpai Village, Dahua Town

Retaining Walls of Kangli Breeding Professional Cooperative Demonstration Base in Nongxiong Village, Qibainong Township

II. Standardized management has been strengthened and remarkable achievements have been made in the construction of cooperatives

The Project has supported the construction of 11 cooperatives. By the end of 2023，1,258 members（households）had been absorbed，including 732 people who have been lifted out of poverty，accounting for 58.19%；1,233 ethnic minorities，accounting for 98.01%；and 440 women，accounting for 34.98%. The cooperatives have increased the income of their members through methods such as dividend awarding，labor employment，and land lease，cumulatively distributing dividends of RMB 2.396 million yuan，benefiting 1，258 rural households，and providing 38 job positions.

A total of **11** cooperatives have been established under the Project，absorbing **1,258** members（households）

The number of people lifted out of poverty
732
Accounting for 58.19%

The number of ethnic minorities
1,233
Accounting for 98.01%

The number o women
440
Accounting for 34.98%

Dividend awarding
Labor employment
Land lease

Cumulative dividends
RMB **2.396** million yuan

The number of households benefited：
1,258

The number of posts
38

In strengthening the standardized management of cooperatives, the main practices are as follows：

First，a cooperative management system has been established.

The operational mechanisms of the cooperatives' councils and boards of supervisors have been clarified，along with the rights and obligations of the members.

Second，equity shares have been clarified.

Equity certificates have been made and issued to each member, and detailed information regarding members，including their names，sources of shares，and shareholdings，has been publicly displayed on the cooperatives' bulletin boards.

Third，emphasis has been given to the openness of social and financial affairs.

Information related to the cooperatives has been promptly and proactively released through WeChat and bulletin boards.

Fourth，democratic management has been adopted.

As expressed by the cooperative members themselves，"Major decisions are made by the members' assembly，while minor matters are decided by the council."

Fifth，good leaders have been selected.

In line with the "three haves" principle—having the desire for the public good，having capabilities，and having time—cooperative management personnel have been elected by the cooperative members.

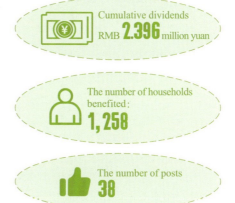

Constitutional Principles of Dahua Nongqu Planting and Breeding Professional Cooperative

Asset Dividend Bulletin Board of Shareholders of Dahua Donghuangling Farmers' Professional Cooperative

III. Professional services have been introduced to improve the quality and efficiency of industrial development

First, professional services have been introduced. Agricultural experts have been invited to the cooperatives for on-site guidance. They have imparted advanced planting techniques and helped achieve standardized and regulated orchard management and care techniques.

Second, production equipment has been improved. The construction and installation of water-fertilizer integrated drip irrigation equipment, compost fermentation equipment, base roller skating track facilities, etc. have significantly improved production efficiency.

Third, financing channels have been improved. By the end of 2023, credit ratings had been completed for 4,000 rural households, and 10 cooperatives had received asset appraisal services.

Fourth, commercial insurance has been purchased. By the end of 2023, insurance had been purchased for 225 mu of Orah mandarin, 15,200 broiler chickens, 5,340 pigs, 512 goats, and 60 cattle, improving the risk prevention capabilities of cooperatives.

On-site Guidance of Agricultural Experts on Techniques such as Planting, Pruning, and Pest Control

Composting Shed of Dahua Donghuangling Farmers' Professional Cooperative

Staff of a Rural Commercial Bank Visiting the Business Incubation Center of Dahua Yao Autonomous County to Negotiate Financing Channel Development with the World Bank-Financed Project Pilot Cooperatives

Insurance Policies for Beef Cattle Breeding and Goat Breeding

IV. Product certification has been conducted and marketing channels have been expanded

By the end of 2023, the Project had supported cooperatives to obtain 4 certifications including green food certification and complete packaging design and trademark registration, thereby increasing the market competitiveness of the cooperatives' products, and addressing the issue of high-quality products not fetching good prices. For instance, Dahua Donghuangling Orah Mandarin Planting Cooperative, which cultivates 225 mu of Orah mandarin, registered the Donghuangling Orah Mandarin trademark in 2018, received green food certification in 2019, and obtained Shenzhen Standard certification in 2020. The sales price of Donghuangling Orah mandarin is 30% higher than other Orah mandarin brands, leading to a yearly increase in its sales revenue.

By the end of 2023, a total of 540 people received planting and breeding technology training, operation and management training, e-commerce livestreaming training to improve the operation and management capabilities of rural households, cooperatives, and local enterprises. Moreover, business incubation centers supported cooperatives and enterprises to participate in offline agricultural product trade fairs held in places like Nanning, reach collaboration intents with numerous enterprises and individuals, and broaden their sales channels.

Green Food Certificate of a Cooperative in Dahua Yao Autonomous County

The Orah Mandarin of Donghuangling Farmers' Professional Cooperative in Zhongwu Village, Duyang Town, Dahua Yao Autonomous County Obtaining Shenzhen Standard Certification

V. Talent training has been strengthened to promote the sustainable development of cooperatives

The World Bank-Financed Project in Dahua Yao Autonomous County has cumulatively participated in and hosted 15 sessions of project training, with a total of 600 participants; it has also organized 2 field investigations with a total of 56 participants, who visited World Bank project cooperatives and industrial bases in Hunan Province and Guizhou Province for study and investigation.

Representatives of World Bank-Financed Project in Dahua Yao Autonomous County Visiting Hunan Province for Study and Investigation

Dahua Yao Autonomous County actively cultivates its characteristic agricultural products. The picture shows a member of Dahua Donghuangling Farmers' Professional Cooperative picking Orah mandarin

Afterword

The photo album was compiled by the Foreign Capital Project Development Center, Rural Revitalization Administration of Guangxi Zhuang Autonomous Region. A wealth of pictures were provided by all levels of Project Management Offices, Tiandong County Rural Revitalization Information Center, Publicity Department of the CPC Pingguo Municipal Committee, Leye County Convergence Media Center, Publicity Department of the CPC Tianlin County Committee, Donglan County Convergence Media Center, Culture and Tourism Bureau of Bama Yao Autonomous County, Publicity Department of the CPC Du'an Yao Autonomous County Committee, and Nanning Honglin Cultural Communication Co., Ltd., as well as enterprises and cooperatives supported by the Project. The Publicity Department of the CPC Yizhou District Committee in Hechi City provided the picture on the cover of the album. All of these pictures laid a solid foundation for the album's smooth compilation and publication.

The content of this photo album involves various aspects of the implementation of the World Bank-Financed Project and spans a significant period of time. The task of compiling this album is substantial, and the abilities of the compilers are also limited. Therefore, if there are any omissions or improprieties, we kindly ask you to provide your criticism and corrections.

Compilation Team

May 2024